Landfall Walks Bo

Bob Acto

AROUND PERRANPORTH, ST AGNES & PORTREATH

The Lappa Valley in winter (Walk 1)

First published 2005
by
LANDFALL PUBLICATIONS
Landfall, Penpol, Devoran, Truro, Cornwall TR3 6NR
Telephone: 01872 862581

ISBN 1 873443 50 1

Typesetting, maps, sketches and recent photographs are by Bob Acton unless otherwise stated.
Maps reproduced by permission of Ordnance Survey on behalf of HMSO.
© Crown Copyright 2005. All rights reserved.
Ordnance Survey Licence number 100024943.

Printed by the Troutbeck Press and bound by R. Booth Ltd,
Antron Hill, Mabe, Penryn, Cornwall

ACKNOWLEDGEMENTS

I began researching walks in the area covered by this book back in 1989, and the list of people who have generously given me their help during the succeeding years is lengthy. It includes several who sadly have now died. Leslie Douch, former Curator of the County Museum, Truro, and the leading authority on East Wheal Rose, checked my typescript of Walk 1; Clive Benney, Margaret Bunt, Isobel Hedges, Trevor Greenslade and Philip Childs gave information about St Agnes; Rose Lewis was immensely helpful regarding Mineral Tramways routes; James Olds told me about Menadarva, Colin Trezise about the Hell's Mouth area, Linda Miners about Perranporth and Michael Tangye about Portreath and Illogan parish; Gill Jacobs provided me with a sort of "Which? Guide to the Best Pubs and Other Places of Refreshment"; Kenneth Brown gave copious information on mines; Roger Glanville and Ron Grubb shared their knowledge of Rose and district with me; and the Secretary of the St Agnes Museum Trust, Roger Radcliffe, meticulously corrected my inaccuracies in early editions and supplied dozens of extra points of interest. I am grateful, too, to all the people I met *en route* or have chatted to over the telephone, who supplied innumerable useful "snippets". My late wife, Viv, provided ideas, information, and companionship on the walks, and my present wife, Stephanie, has been no less enthusiastic and helpful.

CONTENTS

PLEASE NOTE

All these walks are, to the best of my knowledge, on public rights of way. For your own safety, keep to the official paths in mining areas and on clifftops. If you take a good torch on the walks, you will have several opportunities to explore adits and caves, but please take great care: roof-falls are not unknown, and tides have a nasty habit of coming in...

Every effort has been made to check that the information in this book is accurate, but the author cannot accept responsibility for any loss, disappointment, damage or injury caused by reliance on the directions or other details or statements herein.

INTRODUCTION

This book aims to provide a selection of round walks which can be enjoyed by all, and at the same time to give information about the interesting details along the way. The main focus is on the old mines and associated industries such as mineral railways, and there are few areas in Cornwall, or indeed in the world, where the surviving evidence of these things is more plentiful and spectacular. Other features of the area covered are also included in the directions and italicised notes, such as the churches, famous local people, and ancient archaeological sites.

Using the Book

Before you set off, please read the introductory remarks for the walk in question, which will give you some hints about such things as the sort of footwear needed, and whether you will be able to find refreshments on the walk. In some cases, too, you could increase the pleasure of the walk by making prior arrangements, such as telephoning for permission to visit certain sites.

Directions are given in **bold type**, and the lengthier notes on points of interest in *italics*. On pages 155-8 there is a glossary explaining the mining terms used in the book, and on pages 159-60 a list of books consulted and referred to in the text.

The book has a waterproof cover and will fit easily when open into the sort of clear polythene bag used in supermarkets to wrap fruit and vegetables ... so there's no need for rainy weather to prevent you from doing the walks. The sketch maps give only a rough idea of the route, but you should be in no danger of going astray if you follow carefully the very detailed directions. Even so, if you can take along the relevant Ordnance Survey Landranger, Pathfinder or - best of all - Explorer map your understanding of what you see will be further enhanced, and you will have the opportunity to explore this splendid region for yourself.

AROUND PERRANPORTH, ST AGNES & PORTREATH

The walks and other information in this book are based on parts of several earlier publications (*A View from St Agnes Beacon, A View from Carn Brea, Around St Agnes & Perranporth, Exploring Cornish Mines* and *Exploring Cornwall's Tramway Trails*). All the routes have been re-walked during the winter and early spring of 2004-5, and the "points of interest" have all been revised in the light of later events and research.

WALK 1
ST NEWLYN EAST & EAST WHEAL ROSE
About 3 miles

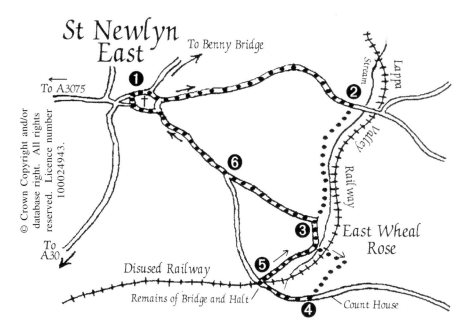

East Wheal Rose was in its day the most important lead mine in Cornwall, and the ruined engine house is the largest and among the most impressive in the county. It stands on land owned by the Lappa Valley Railway, and between Easter and the end of September and on certain days in October you can visit the site by being a passenger on the miniature railway which runs (between 10.15 a.m. and 5.30 p.m.) from the station at Benny Bridge, which is not on the walk route. The phone number for enquiries is 01872 510317.

A detailed account of a tour of East Wheal Rose and neighbouring mines, together with photographs and maps, is in *Exploring Cornish Mines*, Volume 3. If you come to Benny Bridge armed with a copy, you will be given a ticket at reduced price. The St Newlyn East Local Studies Group has produced three excellent publications, a detailed history of the parish and two books of photographs, old and new. If you have difficulty obtaining any of these, ring 01872 510899.

The walk suggested, which gives you a fairly distant but still impressive view of the mine buildings, is quite a short one, including country roads and a most attractive valley path beside a stream. Parts of the path are likely to be muddy.

Shops are available at St Newlyn East, and the Pheasant Inn, near the church, offers good bar food.

To drive to St Newlyn East from St Agnes, take the B3285 to Goonhavern via Perranporth. At Goonhavern turn left on to the Newquay road (A3075), and after about three miles turn right, just past Rejerrah. To drive from Truro, you first need to get to the A30. You could use the main roads (A390 westwards and turn right at Chiverton Cross, or A3076 north and turn left at Carland Cross), but pleasanter would be to go up Kenwyn Road and follow the B3284 as far as Shortlanesend, there forking right on to a minor road to join the A30 south of Zelah. Turn right, and about a mile past Zelah fork left, signposted Newlyn East. After another mile turn right, as signposted. In the village, turn right at the T-junction. You should find room to park near the church.

ST NEWLYN EAST CHURCH

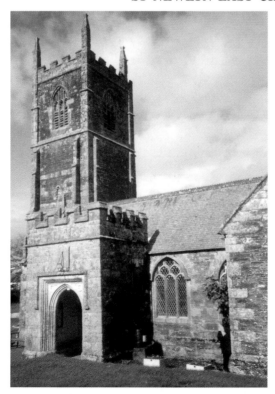

The fig tree, above, can also just be seen on the right side of the larger photograph.

WALK 1

St Newlina's church dates from the late 12th century. The fig tree growing out of its south wall is said to have sprung up when the saint struck the ground with her staff, saying, "Let a church be built." (Manaccan church, near Helford, boasts a similarly surprising fig, and by what appears to be a strange coincidence the noted Cornish historian, Richard Polwhele, was the vicar of Manaccan for 25 years before, as A.L.Rowse puts it, "acquiring the better living of Newlyn East". During at least the last 10 of his 17 years as vicar here [1821-38] he actually resided at his family's estate of Polwhele on the edge of Truro, leaving the nitty-gritty at Newlyn to a series of curates.) Please treat the tree with care: anyone who harms it is doomed to die within a year. The saint herself, who may be the same person as Saint Noluen, patron of Noyale Pontivy in Brittany, is supposed to have met an untimely end by beheading; a 15th-century Lantern Cross near the font portrays a woman holding her head in her arms.

Parts of the chancel and north transept, plus the font, are Norman, and the aisles seem to be 14th- and 15th-century workmanship. The tower was added in the 15th century. The old bench ends at the front of the nave remain, and parts of the medieval rood screen were incorporated in the new one when the church was restored in 1883 - a restoration which, unusually, earns John Betjeman's approval in "Cornwall: A Shell Guide". Under the church is a vault in which were laid to rest seventeen members of the Arundell family, whose nearby Tudor manor house, Trerice, is now owned by the National Trust, and is a "must" for all visitors to this area. "Around Newquay" includes a walk based on Trerice.

1 Radiating from the church is a somewhat confusing multiplicity of roads. Perhaps the best way to direct you is from the church's main entrance, the south porch. Leaving the building at this point, turn right, and at the road right again. At the next T-junction, the Pheasant Inn faces you. This first opened as an ale house in 1842; its original name was The Hawkins Arms: much of the land in the parish belongs to the Trewithen Estate, owned then by the Hawkins family. In 1905 the ale house was bought by a devout Methodist who named it The Temperance Hotel. It became a fully-licensed pub in 1952. **Here once more turn right, and then fork right along Metha Road, ignoring the left turning signposted to Trerice.** The Old Vicarage, on the right at the start of Metha Road, dates in part from the early 18th century, having been rebuilt after a fire in 1728. It was replaced by a smaller vicarage in 1985, and is now divided into flats. 150 years ago the old cottages on the left further along, Metha Row, were mostly occupied by miners, who were granted the privilege of keeping animals on Newlyn Downs. According to the WI's book of Cornish villages, the right to do so still appears on the deeds of these cottages. A little further on again, those tall enough to see over the hedge on the left have a long view stretching to Newquay and the sea.

After a little over half a mile, this attractive country road dips into the Lappa Valley, and you take the signed footpath starting at a stile on the right - but first it's worth continuing downhill for another hundred yards to Metha Bridge, where there are in fact two bridges, the second being over what was originally a mineral railway built by J.T. Treffry. It later became part of the G.W.R., and is now the Lappa Valley miniature steam railway.

TREFFRY'S MINERAL RAILWAY

Joseph Thomas Treffry (pronounced to rhyme with "reply") was one of Cornwall's most daring and imaginative entrepreneurs. His main business interests were in the St Austell china-clay area, and he built Par harbour; his viaduct-cum-aqueduct in the Luxulyan valley is most spectacular. (See "From the Roseland to St Austell Bay" and "Around the River Fowey" for walks exploring these.) In 1837 he bought a small village on the north coast, named after a "new quay" which had been built at least as far back as the 15th century. He developed Newquay's harbour and built a railway for horse-drawn wagons to connect it with his clay pits near St Dennis. In 1849 an extension was added, to East Wheal Rose. In 1873 these "tramways" were bought up by the Cornwall Minerals Railway, converted for use by steam locomotives, and this branch was extended to Treamble to serve the iron mines there: see Walk 5. But there was less demand for the railway's services than had been expected, and before long the lines were taken over by the Great Western Railway in order to complete their route from Chacewater to Newquay. The Treamble branch was used during World War II for troop movements to and from Penhale Camp at Holywell. The Chacewater-Newquay line was eventually axed by Beeching in 1963. Unfortunately, the chance to convert it into an attractive footpath was missed. Lewis Reade's "Branch Line Memories" contains a special feature on the Chacewater to Newquay branch line. Since so many of the walks in this book follow or cross its former track, reading his account and studying his photographs would, I'm sure, enhance your enjoyment. His later volume, devoted entirely to Cornwall, is also worth having.

2 Return to the footpath, which runs beside the stream - very close to it in places, so you must expect mud underfoot. It is also rather uneven, and a little scrambling is needed here and there. This is a lovely wooded valley (Metha Woods), a carpet of bluebells in May and of leaves in the late autumn.

Although the water in the stream always seems to be clear, the bed has the kind of reddish tinge I associate with deposits of ochre, as seen for example in the Carnon River between Twelveheads and Bissoe - and see the note on Red Rivers on page 147.

Soon after the old quarry you have a glimpse of the stack and engine house of East Wheal Rose; but growth of trees now obscures much of the view in my 1989 sketch.

WALK 1

You cross stone and wooden stiles, and then the path curves right. Cross the stile by the metal gate and walk up the farm track to the road.

EAST WHEAL ROSE

East Wheal Rose is one of the few Cornish mines to have had a whole book devoted to it: see the Further Reading list. The maps, diagrams and photographs it contains, as well as Leslie Douch's fascinating account of the mine's history, would add greatly to your enjoyment of this walk.

There were already old workings on a site about two miles west (marked Deerpark Mine on the O.S. Explorer map) when exploratory shafts were sunk in 1812, and it was at once clear that the sett was rich in silver as well as lead. Soon, John Giddy, an employee at the tin-smelting works at Calenick (see "A History of Truro" Volume 3, Country Walk 3) was brought in to manage the mine and set up a lead-smelting house. A residence was built for him at Shepherds, south west of Fiddlers Green. By 1823 the enterprise was making a good profit, but as the shafts went deeper, the quantity and quality of both lead and silver declined. So did the price of lead, and Old Wheal Rose was abandoned at the end of 1832.

A new venture started further east, in the valley of the little River Lappa, in 1834; this proved very productive. "Today," writes Douch, "it is difficult to imagine the scene in the valley when the boom was at its height and the transformation of a quiet stream bed where nothing more mechanical than a water-mill had worked - to the clatter and noise, the hissing and blowing, the bustle and seeming confusion of East Wheal Rose, with over a thousand men, women and children at work, wagons rolling in laden with timber and coals, rolling out with lead ore for the local smelters or the ports, the adit water running heavy and red right down to the Gannel (Newquay)."

In July 1846 occurred a disaster, the worst in Cornish mining history: 38 miners drowned when a cloudburst flooded the workings. Detailed and harrowing accounts of what happened are included by Alan Bennett in "Images of Cornwall" and Cyril Noall in "Cornish Mine Disasters". (About five years later a local Methodist preacher argued that a memorial to the victims was needed, and in response a preaching pit similar to the famous one at Gwennap was created out of a disused quarry. Known simply as The Pit, it is on the south side of Cargoll Road, which leads westwards out of the village, towards Cubert and Holywell.)

The great 100-inch engine house sketched in 1989, before the ivy was removed

The mining was always difficult: the lode was so soft that in 1850 the Mining Journal described it as "literally a quicksand"; "a complete forest of Norway fir has been stowed away underground" to support the shafts. In 1857, the same journal called East Wheal Rose "an exceedingly dangerous (mine) in which to work, probably the most so in the world."

The coming of Treffry's tramroad in 1849 helped to revive the mine's fortunes, but production declined, and the expense of pumping increased as the levels grew deeper, so despite evidence of very rich lead deposits below the 170-fathom level, the underground mining stopped in 1857, although metal went on being recovered profitably from the halvans (waste tips). Most of the buildings that housed engines during the 1840s and '50s were on the site now covered by the landscaped rubbish tip.

In 1881, new adventurers set about mining the deeper ore, and they put to work a very big pumping engine (a new 90-inch one manufactured by Harvey & Co. of Hayle) at Penrose's Shaft; the splendid ruins of the base of its engine house stand on high ground a little way south of this walk route. At about the same time the most powerful beam engine ever to work in Cornwall (which had a cylinder 100 inches in diameter, and had been made, also by Harvey's, for Great Wheal Vor, west of Helston, in 1853) was purchased and installed in a magnificent new engine house at North Wheal Rose Shaft, with a chimney 100 feet high beside it. (Perhaps the height of the stack was symbolic.) The bob (beam) alone of the engine weighed 55 tons. The cost of all the new machinery was never recovered, and in 1885, just before the crucial 170-fathom level was reached, East Wheal Rose finally closed. The 100-inch engine, which had worked in Wales before coming here, was sold and taken to Millom in Cumbria. The engine house itself now belongs to a local educational trust, which has the responsibility of maintaining it.

My original note in the first edition of this book ended as follows: "Mrs Booth, the owner of the miniature railway, tells me that the last remnants of the roof fell in during spring 1988, and that there are many other signs of deterioration; urgent action would seem to be needed to preserve this building, which is surely of national importance." I am delighted to be able to add that such action has now been taken.

3 Turn left. Soon you pass the ancient-looking, slate-hung farmhouse at Nanhellan. (Eleven households at Nanhellan hamlet were associated with mining according to the 1851 census.) **About a hundred yards beyond the farmhouse, take the public footpath on the left signposted to East Wheal Rose. It leads to a footbridge, and then a few steps up bring you to the trackbed of the disused railway, now occupied by the miniature railway's extension to its southern terminus at "Newlyn Halt". Cross that with care and then climb more steps to what was, back in 1989 when I wrote** *A View from St Agnes Beacon***, a vast refuse tip.** Since then it has been closed to further dumping, and landscaped so successfully that it's hard to imagine now the ugliness and desolation that so recently characterised this area. It's now Newlyn East Golf Course (9 holes). Gates and fencing on the left discourage trespass in that direction, tempting though that may be for those who want a closer view of the great engine house. A second change affecting the place since I originally researched this walk is nearly as dramatic as the first: it results from the creation of a "wind farm" at Carland Cross. The tall windmills, though a mile away, dominate the view, and on the day I last did this walk the breeze carried to my ears a constant sound as of a distant stormy sea. **The path runs between tall hedges at first - protection from bombardment by golf balls! - then goes downhill to a wooden stile. Cross that and turn right on the gravelled track, which eventually joins the road at a stile on the left-hand side of a pair of large metal gates - once the main entrance to the tip.**

4 Turn right at the road. On your left now is Penhallow Moor, scarred by the remains of other lead mines, notably Wheal Constance and Cargoll Mine. Soon you cross the stream again. Next come the remains of a bridge which carried the old railway, and the small path up the bank on the left on the far side leads to a tiny platform with a battered corrugated-iron shelter, melancholy monuments to Dr Beeching. This was once Mitchell and Newlyn Halt - "a railway archaeology site well worth a visit," as Lewis Reade says, but a notice forbids access to it now. Photographs of it in its working days and as it is now are in all three of the Local Studies Group's books. (See Further Reading.)

5 Turn right just beyond the railway bridge, along a narrow road heading towards East Wheal Rose engine house. For the rest of the round walk as shown on the sketch map, keep to this road as it bends left at Nanhellan, then runs uphill between high hedges. (Admittedly, this part of the walk is rather uninspiring, so you might prefer to retrace your earlier steps from Nanhellan, back through the Lappa Valley and along Metha Road to the village.)

6 Continuing with the round walk: at the T-junction (Ventonarren Farm) turn right. This, for the reason you now know, is called Halt Road; before that it was Mine Lane, for another reason you now know. It soon brings you back to the church.

If you want to take a trip on the miniature railway and inspect the mine buildings at close quarters, drive or walk up the road signposted to Trerice, which is the left turn near the start of the walk I have described. The railway terminus is at Benny Bridge.

WALK 2
VENTONGIMPS, CALLESTICK & THE CHIVERTON MINES
About 5 miles, or a 6-mile version, starting and ending at a pub

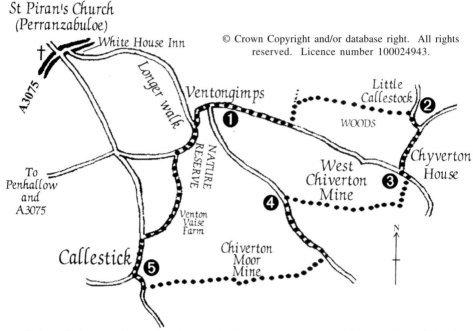

St Piran's Church
(Perranzabuloe)
White House Inn

West Chiverton's engine house is just as unusual as that of East Wheal Rose, and almost as imposing; it illustrates well the builders' pride in their work. The walk also includes the remains of a smaller lead mine, and passes through the beautiful estates of Chyverton House. You could visit the famous gardens (by prior arrangement: see the directions), and also inspect a nature reserve at Ventongimps.

About half of the route is on very quiet roads; the rest is tracks and paths through woodland and open fields. There are many muddy patches - in fact this is definitely a "welly walk", except perhaps during a long drought. The optional section through woodland early in the walk involves either a quite steep and slippery descent or some scrambling over and around fallen trees, and stepping over some barbed wire, but you are unlikely to have any serious difficulties. There is no shop on this walk, but the longer route starts and ends at an inn which does good food. During the season you could visit Callestock Cyder Farm to sample their scrumpy and find out about the art of cider making.

14

WALK 2

The shorter version of this walk starts and ends at Ventongimps.
To drive there from St Agnes, take the B3285 (Perranporth) road. After less than two miles turn right on to minor roads which take you through Mithian to join the A3075 (Newquay) road just south of Penhallow. Turn left and then first right (immediately beyond the Plume of Feathers pub). Continue ahead at the next crossroads.

To drive from Truro, take the A390 westwards; at the big Chiverton roundabout, where it meets the A30, turn right on to the A3075 Newquay road. At the Plume of Feathers in Penhallow, about three miles further on, turn right for Ventongimps. Continue ahead at the next crossroads.

There is not much room to park in the village. If you turn right, over the 17th-century bridge and past what remains of the old watermill, you may find space on the left after a few yards, but please avoid blocking any entrances. A little further up, the road widens somewhat just before a house on the left, and this is probably the best spot for a parked car or two.

For the longer version, continue along the A3075 to Perranzabuloe; the church is on the left, and on the right is the White House Inn, whose owners have kindly given me permission to suggest that you park there. The Inn is noted for good food, so it makes an ideal ending for a walk. It stands at a corner where a country road joins the A3075; to start from there, walk along this quiet road. After about half a mile it brings you to Ventongimps. Turn left over the bridge.

VENTONGIMPS

The name means "level spring" (Cornish, fenten compes); Oliver Padel suggests that "level" refers to the flow of the water. It's certainly a watery place, with its stream running through a marshy valley, into which the water collecting underground at the nearby lead mines flows via at least one adit. Well up the valley a leat used to take water from the stream to power two waterwheels - one overshot and one undershot - at what was, at least until the start of the 20th century, an imposing three-storey manorial corn mill, attached to the miller's cottage or cottages. (Apparently there were two dwellings originally.) "Fentengempes" or "Fentergempys" Mill is mentioned in documents as far back as 1330 and 1413. In later centuries it became known as "Shewsy's Mill". The present owner of the former mill barn, now converted into an attractive house, told me the mill was sold, many years ago, to a scrap merchant who proceeded to gut it, not only of all the machinery but of every saleable item including the wooden beams - hence the sad condition it is now in (early 2005), not only derelict but relying on at least one massive wooden buttress to stave off final collapse.

1 From the suggested parking places at Ventongimps, continue up this country road for about half a mile. A signed public bridleway on the edge of woodland meets the road here, going off both left and right. To visit the lead mine sites you could simply go on along the road, and continue following the directions from point 3; but for an attractive walk through open farmland, woods and the Chyverton House estate, take the left-hand track. (Bear in mind, though, the remarks about this optional section of the walk in the introduction.) **After about 150 yards, follow the track among trees on the right. Soon - just beyond a metal farm gate - the track bears right, into an open field, but you need to keep straight on. The path runs between two low walls, or "hedges".** (In Cornwall the word "hedge" is often used to refer to dry-stone walling; such walls are filled with earth, and after a short time the stone is usually almost hidden by plant growth, as well as providing homes for vast numbers of insects and other small animal life.) **After a little less than 150 yards, the way ahead is blocked by shrubby growth, and here you bear right, keeping fairly near the hedge on your right at first. The path is not very clear, but if you stay in the woodland and keep going roughly straight ahead you will soon descend into a small valley. The obvious way, a little to the right, is a steep and usually slippery path; if you prefer to avoid that you will probably have to scramble over and duck under fallen trees on the way down. At the bottom are two streams, both heavily stained with red ochre (iron oxide), fairly conclusive evidence that the water issues from a mine adit. There used to be two footbridges, one of granite and the other of wood/earth, but the stone one is no longer usable. Having crossed, go up slightly to the right, where you need to step over a low barbed-wire fence.** (Some wood has been attached, presumably to make things easier, but I'm not convinced it succeeds. "Is this a walk or an assault course?" I hear you cry.) **Now walk across the open field (almost straight on - very slightly left) and through the metal farm gate (yellow waymark arrow) at the corner of the hedge of the next field. From here to the road at Little Callestock the path is obvious, running on the left side of the hedge.**

2 At the road, turn right, and then bear right on the pretty road through the Chyverton estate. Chyverton House can be glimpsed on the left as you approach the T-junction, where you turn left.

CHYVERTON HOUSE

The name (pronounced "Chiverton") seems to mean "the house on the grassland". The original farmhouse, part of the huge Arundell estate, was replaced by the present mansion about 1781. For many years it belonged to the Thomas family, prominent in Cornish mining concerns, and they developed the large garden, landscaped in the Georgian manner with lake and bridge. In 1820 it was described as displaying "many beauties, consisting of neat sheets of water, fine gardens, and thriving plantations". Since 1924, under the ownership of the Cornish engineering family, the Holmans, it has been further enhanced by a large collection of exotic shrubs and trees, the magnolias being particularly famous. The books by Bill Trembath and Douglas Ellory Pett give detailed information about the garden and its plants. The garden is private, but between March and June group visits may sometimes be arranged by appointment (tel. 01872-540324).

3 After a few yards, just before the main entrance to Chyverton, turn right on to a wide but bumpy and muddy track. Soon this bends sharply right; follow it round, ignoring the left turnings, and you now come to the surviving buildings of West Chiverton Mine.

 The old building over to the right at first (shown in the foreground in this 1989 photo) is what remains of the boiler house for the stamps engine; the engine house itself was demolished half a century ago.

WALK 2

When I originally researched this book, in 1989, the big pumping-engine house was surrounded by huge mine-waste tips. By 1993 the area had been designated a "landfill site", and the landscape was undergoing drastic transformation by the agency of lorries and earth-movers. Now (January 2005) all is quiet again and natural vegetation is gradually re-establishing itself. **The engine house can be approached by means of a track on the far side (yellow waymark arrow), at the start of which is a metal gate.**

WEST CHIVERTON MINE

Apart from East Wheal Rose, this was Cornwall's most important lead mine, and it also produced nearly one and a quarter million ounces of silver. Its main period of activity was between 1859 and 1886, and the amount of waste material dumped showed how busy a mine it was; in 1870 it was employing 1,000 people. A large quantity of zinc was recovered from the dumps after the mining had ceased.

The engine house at Batter's Shaft is particularly impressive, being three storeys high and built with unusual attention to detail, as illustrated in the sketch, below right.

18

In 1869 an 80-inch pumping engine was installed here, made by Harvey & Co. of Hayle; it was reputed to be an exceptionally fine one. After the mine closed it was moved to United Mines at Gwennap, and later to Great Condurrow near Camborne. At both sites its house is still

Picnic-time at Batter's Shaft

visible. The builders at West Chiverton made the task of installing and removing the huge engine harder by placing the stack at the centre of the wall opposite the bob wall; nearly all other houses had a large opening at this point for that purpose: to use a side entrance was much more awkward. The unusual design was said to be to make the east wall of the house, with its huge "cylinder doorway" and arched windows, impressive when seen by visitors and shareholders of the mine calling at the count house. On the east side of the engine house was the reservoir where the "tailings" (waste materials suspended in water) were put to settle out, and beyond that were the dressing floors and the stamps: as previously mentioned, the stamps-engine house was eventually blown up (in 1952, and without warning, much to the disgust of all who valued Cornwall's mining heritage), but the boiler house and some fragments of the engine house remain. Old photos showing the stamps-engine house and the huge area of dumps are in L.J.Bullen's Volume 5. (See Further Reading.)

After inspecting the engine house, return through the gate to the main track. As you continue the walk you have a good view southwards, and can just make out among trees the ruined engine house of Chiverton Moor Mine, which the walk is now heading for. **The track curves left as it reaches the road.**

4 Turn left on the road, and after about a quarter of a mile go through a five-bar wooden farm gate on the right, which comes about fifty

yards before the hedge between two quite large fields. (In case you are in doubt: the gate in question is set back about 10 yards from the road, and when we last did this walk was secured at the bottom-left corner with a short length of chain.) **Walk straight down the slope, parallel with the hedge to your left. At the bottom, close to the corner of the field, cross the footbridge and go through the small wooden gate. Now go straight across the next field, heading for the ruined engine house. Go through the gap beside a battered metal farm gate by a small stream. The path to follow now runs on the right side of the hedge in front of you.**

Now you will soon come to the remaining bob wall (i.e. the thickest wall of the engine-house, which supported the weight of the bob or beam of the pumping engine) of Chiverton Moor Mine. The site is now badly overgrown (more so, in fact, than when this photo was taken, in 1989), but the hollows and hillocks in quite an extensive area, mainly to the west, are obvious relics of its spoil-heaps.

CHIVERTON MOOR MINE

An ancient mine, known once as Great Callestock Moor, this was a much smaller enterprise than West Chiverton, producing about 2,240 tons of lead and 24,000 ounces of silver between 1847 and 1873. The engine house was built about 1863 for a 70-inch beam engine to pump the water from shafts which had reached 500 feet in depth by 1870. Another engine house, now apparently gone without trace, contained a winding engine. 150 people were employed here then.

Go on past the ruin for a few yards. Notice, a few feet to the right of the path, what appears to be a cylinder bedstone, a large granite block with four bolts projecting. It is too small to have served a 70-inch engine and may be a relic of the whim (winding engine).

Then bear right, along a few yards of rather overgrown path and through another gap beside a fallen farm gate. Go diagonally across the small field to a gap on the right, which brings you into a bigger field. Walk by the hedge on your left for a few yards, and you will find a metal gate with an old stone stile on its left. If the stile is still unusable because of barbed wire, go through the gate, and now you are on a lane leading direct to Callestick. (No problems with finding your way, but when I was last there the mud was well up to usual West Country standards, especially at the far end.)

5 At the road, in the attractive hamlet of Callestick, turn right.

CALLESTICK
Pronounced as three syllables with the stress on the second one, the name appears also as "Callestock", but Oliver Padel considers it unlikely to be the same in meaning as "Calstock", a name of English origin, as is

true of many place-names in the easternmost part of the county. "Callestick" probably derives from the Cornish language, but its meaning is obscure. Bill Trembath writes of the days when Callestick was populated mainly by miners, and had its own pub, the Albert Inn, which closed in 1893 as a result of the decline of local mining. (The pub building is now a private house bearing the same name, which may refer to the nearby Wheal Albert, visited on Walk 3.) In 1826 the first Wesleyan chapel in the parish was built at Callestick.

Turn right again, signposted to Perran Church and Perranporth.
Callestick Farm, on the corner, is well known throughout Cornwall for its dairy ice cream. To visit the Callestock Cyder Farm, which is normally open from 9 a.m. to 6 p.m. every day except Sunday between March and Christmas, ignore for the moment the right turning to Perran Church; follow the road round past the telephone box. Go straight on up the hill, past the farm house and a chapel. The Cyder Farm is signposted on the left.

If your car is parked at the White House Inn, you could continue along the road signposted to Perran Church, going straight on at the crossroads; you will reach the A3075 just a few yards from the Inn.

To return to Ventongimps, take the first right turning, a narrow, pretty road - little more than a lane, and well laced with mud - which passes the Manse and Venton Vaise ("spring in the open field") farm. Turn right again at the "main" road, which leads into Ventongimps.

On the right before the bridge you will see a notice mentioning that there is a reserve here. It is a SSSI (Site of Special Scientific Interest) belonging to the Cornwall Wildlife Trust. The reserve is open to the public, but waterproof footwear is essential - or bare feet! There are about twenty acres of wet heath, bog and damp woodland, and a pond formed in 1970 when the remains of a crashed World War II bomber were dug out. Many types of butterfly thrive here, including the Marsh Fritillary, which was re-introduced at Ventongimps after becoming rare in the West Country. It also seems likely that snipe and quail are breeding in the reserve; but the main interest is to botanists, since the mosaic of wet and dry areas has encouraged unusual plants such as the Dorset Heath to flourish. More information can be obtained from the board near the entrance and from the Trust at Five Acres, Allet, Truro (01872-273939).

WALK 3
BOLINGEY, NEW CHIVERTON, WHEAL ALBERT
& ST PIRAN'S ROUND

About 7 miles - or a little 2-mile walk based on Bolingey

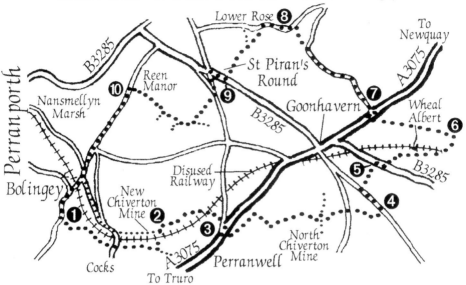

Bolingey, a very pretty old village, has a general store and a nice, cosy pub, the Bolingey Inn. The first half of the route runs alongside a disused railway. If you do the full walk you will see the remains of several mines, two of which still have engine houses, although both are in an advanced state of decay. Near the end of the walk is an impressive, well-preserved ancient fort and "playing place". Most of the route is on well-made, though usually muddy, tracks; one part, around Wheal Albert, is marshy, and on that part of the walk in winter or during a wet spell you would almost certainly need wellington boots. Near the half-way point on the walk you could, during the season, visit "The World in Miniature", which features accurate models of famous buildings, statues and other marvels from all over the world. There is a cafeteria on the site. For those who want only a short, easy walk, a two-mile version is suggested, visiting Bolingey and New Chiverton mine only.

To drive to Bolingey from St Agnes, take the B3285 east to Perranporth, and from there go south on the B3284. After about a mile, Bolingey is signposted to the left.

WALK 3

From Truro, take the A390 westwards to the Chiverton Cross roundabout, then the A3075 towards Newquay, and then turn left on to the B3284 to Perranporth. As you reach the outskirts of Perranporth, turn right where signposted to Bolingey.

In the village, turn right at the T-junction, passing the Bolingey Inn, and you should find room to park on the left just before Bolingey Lake.

BOLINGEY

The name means "mill house" and appears elsewhere in Cornwall in such forms as "Mellingey", "Melinsey" and possibly also "Valency". (The stream that flows past the New Chiverton engine house is called the Mellingey or Molingy, and there is a Mellingey Cottage a mile or so up-stream in Penwartha Coombe: see Walk 4.) A photograph showing the two overshot waterwheels at Bolingey Mill (on the route of this walk, near the end) is in D.E.Benney's "Cornish Watermills", and it is presumably the same mill that used to be depicted on the inn sign in the village. (Paintings of engine houses had replaced it by 2005.)

1 Continue in the direction you were driving (past Kernowcraft and The Old Pottery), and then turn left over a bridge. At first you are among houses. Where the track divides, fork left. The track now takes you through an attractive little valley dominated by a hill which was ablaze with gorse in March. After passing the lake you reach a road, with the hamlet of Cocks on the right. Continue on the attractive public footpath opposite. Go over the stone stile on the left side of a gate, but when you come to a second gate don't cross the stile beside that one: follow the left-hand of the two yellow waymarker arrows to a lower stile a few feet away. You now cross a small stream by stepping stones and a larger one by a bridge, then go under the viaduct which once carried the loop line from Chacewater to Newquay via Mount Hawke, St Agnes, Goonbell, Mithian, Perranporth, Goon-havern, the Lappa Valley and Trewerry & Trerice (see Walks 1 and 9 and *Around*

Newquay for details)**, over another small bridge, and after a few steps down a wall the path runs uphill to meet a wider track.**

2 Here you could turn left to have a look at the engine house of New Chiverton mine; the path passes beside the fenced, open New Engine Shaft, and the ivy-covered engine house stands about twenty feet above.

A photograph of this engine house as it was in 1935 is in H.G.Ordish's 1967 volume. The view here was taken in 1993; the building is even more overgrown now.

The house nearby was originally the mine's count house, and there are also the remains of what may have been the miners' dry.

NEW CHIVERTON MINE

This mine, otherwise known as Old Wheal Anne, had a 40-inch pumping engine in 1864. (Ordish refers to a 52-inch engine; whether this replaced the 40-inch or was in addition I don't know.) In 1870 the mine was employing 50 people. Between 1864 and its closure in 1878 it produced

300 tons of lead, 640 tons of zinc, a little iron and arsenic, and 1,300 ounces of silver. Many local people know New Chiverton as Calley Mine - or perhaps that name is more accurately applied only to the section at New Engine Shaft. An article by Alice M. Bizley in "Old Cornwall" (Autumn 1983) refers to an old man whose father could remember when the boiler was taken out at Calley: a team of 22 horses was required to draw it away. The ghosts that are supposed to haunt the mine at night may, Mrs Bizley suggests, be the barn owls that live in the engine house. A proposal to stabilise the engine house in 1999 met with local opposition on the grounds that three species of bat have colonised it, and "the surrounding area had regenerated into one rich in wildlife over the past 50 years". There was certainly no sign, early in 2005, that any work had been done on the building.

For the short walk, continue ahead down the valley, and at the road still go on in the same direction. Keep to the lower road, ignoring the right fork, and after about another quarter of a mile you will reach a crossroads; Mill Road, on the left, will take you back into Bolingey, as described near the start of point 10.

To continue the full walk, return along the same path and keep straight on, crossing a stile on the right of a gate. Eventually the track bears right, skirts a pond and passes under a railway bridge, another relic of the old Chacewater-Newquay branch.

3 At the road - a very busy one, so take care - cross, go a few yards to the right, and then take the byway going sharp left. (But first you might be interested to walk up on the right to the converted Perranwell chapel buildings, dating from 1843 and 1867, rather stranded now at a higher level than the main road. The white wooden building next to them, in use a few years back as a bric-a-brac shop but now becoming derelict, is a surprising survival from the old Nobel Dynamite Works at Cligga Head (Walk 7), purchased in 1918 for £200 as a Sunday School building.) **After the houses, continue ahead along a narrow, often muddy path. (Horses use it.) When this meets a wider track, ignore**

the track going left: **continue ahead, keeping to the main track as it bears right. Fork left before a gate, the entrance to Pensilver Farm. After quite a long, straight, uphill stretch, part of which runs beside the land belonging to the Silverbow Park camping and caravan site, the track curves right and left**. Here there is a small patch of woodland on the left, where the ground seems to have been disturbed by mining, and on the right is a capped shaft. This was North Chiverton mine, and soon you are surrounded by waste tips and capped shafts.

NORTH CHIVERTON MINE

This was opened in 1863, re-working an older mine called Wheal Anna, dating from at least 1836. An illustration of the immense efforts and determination which went into Cornish mining is that to drain these workings a deep adit nearly 5,000 feet long had been dug, starting in the valley near Perranwell. In 1863 a house was built to take a 50-inch engine; by 1867 the main shaft was down to about 700 feet, and 44 people were employed at the mine; but the lode did not fulfil expectations, and work ceased the following year. The sales recorded for those five years were 100 tons of lead ore, 630 tons of blende (zinc sulphide), a little iron and 3,640 ounces of silver.

Ignore the tracks to right and left: take the one that bears slightly right (a yellow waymarker points the way), then left past a pair of cottages converted into one house. You now join a narrow path, cobbled at first but rather muddy later. Before long, this brings you to a road. Cross and continue on the track opposite. This track passes to the left of a house (Higher Polgoda Farm), becomes a path and later joins a wider track.

4 Turn left at the road, and just past the bungalow on the left, take the track on the right signed Greenmeadow Cottages. Over to the right now is the World in Miniature theme park.

5 At the next road, turn right, and take the first track on the left, by a house labelled Tremorna and Harmony Cottage. After the houses (the last of which is named Count House, and therefore seems likely to have belonged to the mine that lies ahead), **go straight on, between wooden fences, and over a wooden stile on the right side of a rickety, rusty and bent gate. Now the path is very boggy, but passable if you choose your route with care.** On the left here, close to the course of the disused railway line, is a small reserve called Carn Moor, cared for by the Cornwall Wildlife Trust; like the Ventongimps reserve nearby (Walk 2) this is a wetland area (you hardly needed to be told!) where pheasants, snipe, herons and buzzards may be seen. **Continue ahead. Soon you reach the ruinous and overgrown engine house of Wheal Albert, where the path is usually at its soggiest.**

WHEAL ALBERT

This was first worked in 1826 under the name of Goonhavern Mine. Renamed Wheal Albert in the 1850s - perhaps as a tribute to royalty, like Prince Royal Mine in Perrancoombe - it was worked with the aid of a 24-inch engine, and in the 1860s a 45-inch one was installed. The ruined engine house is the one built for that. Hamilton Jenkin says the mine closed in 1867, but according to J.H.Collins it was employing 70 people in 1870. The metals recovered were mainly lead and zinc.

Wheal Albert's pumping-engine house. The sketch is based on a 1935 photograph; the photo on the right shows what remained in 2005.

After this, go through a wooden five-bar gate (yellow waymark arrow), then left, through a second similar gate. At this point you are crossing the old railway track. A third gate of the same type bears an arrow pointing right; following that brings you to a wooden stile. Follow the obvious path ahead between gorse patches. Notice the low railway embankment a few feet away to your right, beneath which the stream flows, via a brick-built arch. **Soon you will see another wooden stile. A few steps ahead bring you to a footbridge, after which walk a few more yards beside the little stream and cross a low, mossy wall with the aid of a few steps. Now turn left.**

6 Turn left again at the wide track, which continues for nearly a mile. Another entrance to the Carn Moor nature reserve has been created, giving easy access to a long boardwalk through the marsh: very useful as a picnic stop, we found! **At the road, cross, again taking great care, and turn right.**

7 Next turn left on to a quiet, attractive little road, passing the Newperran Holiday Park and later Paradise Cottage. The farm soon after this is called Wheal Hope, and if you look down to the wooded valley you may be able to make out signs of old mining activity. This was a small lead mine; apparently the hope was not fulfilled, because no record remains of its output. **Not far past the farm, the road curves right; go down the track on the left here. Where the track bends sharp left, go straight on.** The burrow on the right here is probably a legacy of Wheal Hope. **At the next left bend go ahead on to the narrow grassy path which brings you down to the road.**

8 Turn left, crossing the stream by the bridge beside the ford (although a culvert takes the stream underneath the road, so the bridge is needed only in very wet spells). Mr Roger Glanville told me that this place, locally known as "Tommascotty", was another one where water-powered Cornish stamps (for crushing tin ore) once operated: compare the comments on Stampas Farm on page 46. **Then continue up the road till you reach the houses and cottages of Lower Rose.** (There is a note about Rose on page 61.)

Opposite the lane on the right to Lower Town Farm there are two field gates on the left. Go through the right-hand one and walk along the path ahead, on the left edge of the field. Go through the kissing-gate on the left, turn right along the field edge and through a gate to join a lane. This is locally called "Stile Lane": the story goes that at the Lower Rose end of it there were originally steps to help the bearers at walking funerals going to the old parish church in the sands. **Just before you reach the road, cross the stile on your right to visit St Piran's Round.** (The bench on the right before you enter the Round is dedicated

WALK 3

to Roger Glanville, the "Man of Rose" who gave me so much information about this area when I was preparing earlier editions of this book. He died in 2002.)

ST PIRAN'S ROUND

Otherwise known as Piran Round or Perran Round, this was first recorded in 1747 (Martyn's map), but it almost certainly originated as a fortified settlement surrounded by a circular bank of earth and stone which gave protection from the weather and wild animals such as wolves, as well as human enemies. It has been suggested that in Cornwall as many as a thousand such sites were constructed and occupied around the time of the Roman occupation of Britain. In about the 14th and 15th centuries this particular "round" was adapted as one of many medieval amphitheatres in Cornwall where the miracle plays were performed. (Elsewhere they are usually called "Plain an Gwarry" or "Playing Place". The only other one which is anything like as well preserved as this is in the centre of St Just-in-Penwith: see "A View from Carn Galver", Walk 2, or "Around Land's End", Walk 6.) It appears that at Piran Round a second entrance was made, opposite the original one, and steps were cut in the bank to make seats for the audience. Hamilton Jenkin ("Cornwall and its People") writes: "In the bottom .... may still be seen a three-foot pit which perhaps served as the infernal region...." (The pit Jenkin mentions - not exactly three-foot nowadays - is known locally as the Devil's Frying Pan. Tradition says if you run round it seven times and then put your ear to the ground in the middle you can hear the devil frying souls. In addition to, or instead of, representing Hell, it may have been used to create the illusion of people or animals rising from the ground, as for example in the Creation scenes.) "During the performance," he continues, "the position of the actors in the 'plain' itself was carefully orientated. God and Heaven took the east; the Devil and Hell the north; worldly potentates were assigned to the west; whilst saints and good characters occupied the south. 'Distinguished characters,' writes Mr Nance, 'had their own "tents", "palaces" or "towers", probably consisting at the most, of sentry-boxes made of wood.' In some cases Heaven appears to have been represented by a scaffold erected above the plain. In 1575 an entry in the borough accounts of St Ives records: 'Spent upon the carpenters that made hevin, 4d'." Between 1969 and 1973 several performances of the Cornish play-cycle, the Ordinalia, were given at Piran Round; these plays seem to have been written between 1350 and 1500 at Glasney College, Penryn. Betty Roberts, the

Administrator at Piran Round when it was reopened, wrote in the 1973 programme about the drawbacks and advantages of performing in the open air. "St Piran was in the middle of his big speech. 'Give me a sign Oh Lord,' he thundered. 'Give me a sign.' The Lord, very obligingly, I felt, decided to co-operate, and, right on cue, sent a flash of lightning and a roll of thunder."

9 Turn right on the road - another busy one, I'm afraid, but you soon leave it, following the sign to Reen Cross and Perranwell on the left. Before the houses, take the track on the right, where from the gaps in the hedge you have wide, open views. On the skyline ahead is Mithian Church, close to the big Chiverton roundabout on the A30, with the Fourburrow windfarm to its left and, much more distant, the tall Fourlanes mast to its right; further right is St Agnes Beacon, and then comes Perranporth. The houses at Goonhavern and the windfarm at Carland Cross can be seen by looking back to your left when you have gone a few hundred yards along the track. This is "Jack's Lane", called after Jacka's Shaft, which was in a field on the right. The shafts of Budnick Mine, of which this was one, were named after mining families from Rose, including Hooper and Bice. Budnick was at its most prosperous in the first half of the 19th century; there is little left to see of the mine on surface even though it continued in production till 1904, and the area was prospected again between the wars. Copper, tin, lead, silver and zinc were all produced at various periods.

At the T-junction turn right. The lane you join here was once the road from Perranporth to Goonhavern, travelled on foot daily by many schoolchildren at a time when the only school in Perranporth was for infants. Other children went to school in Penwartha Coombe: see page 37. **Ignore the left fork soon after, and carry on past Higher Reen Farm** (notice the fine view of Perranporth from here) **to join the road at Reen Manor.** The local Old Cornwall Society's book, *Perranzabuloe 1900-1985*, describes Reen Manor Farm as "the oldest building in the parish", dating from about 1591.

10 Turn left, and now continue along this pretty little road for about a mile. There are some spectacularly bent trees and bushes - a result of salt-laden winds which stunt growth on the windward side - and a good view over Perranporth to the sea. **Ignore the left turn and descend into the valley. Cross the main road** (but see the note about Nansmellyn

Marsh) **and keep straight on along Mill Road into Bolingey.** The corn mill dates back to at least 1337, and worked till World War 2. In 1973 it was converted into six dwellings. As shown by an old photo in *Perranzabuloe 1900-1985*, its two waterwheels were roughly where the flight of stairs now is. **After the shop, cross two bridges over streams separated by the old railway bridge. Walk on up Penwartha Road and past the Bolingey Inn to return to your car.**

NANSMELLYN MARSH

There is a nature reserve in the care of the Cornwall Wildlife Trust at Nansmellyn ("Mill Valley") Marsh, which you could visit by turning right instead of going along Mill Road into Bolingey. After about a quarter of a mile, take the path on the right at Nansmellyn Farm. The reserve consists of ten or eleven acres covered mostly by willows and reed-beds, and is remarkable as a breeding ground for 58 species of birds and 90 species of butterflies and moths. The river there is full of trout. There is a bird hide on the eastern side, and early in 1994 a new boardwalk leading to that has been constructed with the aid of a grant from Marks & Spencer and the Civic Trust. Visitors who respect the flora and fauna are welcome, but must stay on the paths and keep dogs on leads. Further details can be obtained from the CWT at 5 Acres, Allet, Truro (phone: 01872-273939), and keys for the hide can be hired from the Perranporth Information Centre (01872-573368).

A thatched cottage in Bolingey

WALK 4
PERRANZABULOE CHURCH, BOLINGEY
& PENWARTHA COOMBE
About 3 miles

This is a charming walk, and amazingly varied for so short a route. The main points of interest, apart from the scenery and long views, are the church - less than two centuries old, but much of it salvaged from its medieval predecessor - and the use of water-power in the valley. Mining has also had its effect on this landscape, though this fact is less obvious today than on most other walks in this book.

Pleasant pubs offering good food are conveniently situated at the start-end point (the White House Inn, Penhallow) and half-way (the Bolingey Inn). Bolingey also has a general store. The going is easy throughout, but you have to be prepared to climb or scramble around one or two gates, and waterproof footwear would be essential except in unusually dry spells.

The suggested start-and-end point is Perranzabuloe Parish Church. Directions for driving there from St Agnes or Truro are given at the start of Walk 2. Immediately beyond the church turn left (i.e. north-west, towards Perranporth). There is usually room to park in the layby on the left, but please avoid doing so at times of church services, when you should still be able to park on the left side of the road a little further along.

PERRANZABULOE PARISH CHURCH

The history of this building is a sequel to the events described in the note on St Piran's Oratory, Cross and Church on pages 47-9. As said there, the building of the new church began in 1804; it was consecrated in July 1805. If it looks rather older than that, this is because much of the tower, some window tracery and several inside features were salvaged from the Norman church. Parts of the lychgate, too, were rescued from the church in the sands. Since most of the population of Perranzabuloe parish lives two miles away at Perranporth, a chapel of ease, St Michael's, was built there in 1872. (See page 64.) For more detail, read "The Four Churches of Perranzabuloe", listed under Further Reading.

1 Enter the churchyard by the gate beside the layby and go round the far side of the church to the main entrance, the south door. Notice, close to that, the ancient, small Cornish cross salvaged from St Piran's Oratory before that was reburied under the sands in 1980. (There is a note about the Oratory on pages 47-9.)

To start the walk, take the path leading from the south door, past a seat and the attractive Trembath Garden, a collection of small memorial tablets usually graced with a mass of flowers. The path continues to the right, downhill, beside a Cornish hedge on your left. After a couple of steps down, it continues for a while between hedges to a low stone stile, where you join a wider track. Continue in the same direction. Where the track ends at a gate and an open field, follow the right-hand waymark arrow on the wooden stile. The path now seems to run beside the curving hedge on the right side of the field rather than keeping to a straight line as indicated on the OS map. Cross the granite stile beside a wooden post with another yellow arrow and continue beside the hedge on the right. On the skyline to your right are the windmills at Carland Cross; also to the right but much closer is the quite deep valley in which used to run the branch line from Chacewater to Newquay (details in Walks 1, 3 & 9), and as you continue downhill you will see the engine house of New Chiverton Mine, also visited on Walk 3. **At the bottom corner of this large field the path goes down quite steeply. Ignore the stile on the right and still continue ahead, following the sign marked Bolingey, crossing a granite cattle-grid and still keeping to the field edge. At the corner, go through the old wooden gate on the right, then follow the wide, curving drive (Trevellance Lane) among houses, eventually crossing either the footbridge or the road bridge over the Penwartha stream.**

2 At the road, if you want to visit Bolingey, possibly to get refreshments at the pub or shop, turn right past the entrance to the Bolingey Lake angling club. The Bolingey Inn is only a few hundred yards along the road, but for the shop you need to continue beyond the railway bridge. (By the way, you may, like us, be intrigued by the tall chimney stack rising from a bank near houses behind the pub. It is, we were told, just a domestic chimney, originally belonging to a small hotel, and may have been made so tall in order to reduce the risk of setting fire to the thatched roofs that were close by when it was built.) **Return the same way and go on ahead up the valley road to continue the walk.**

If you don't want to go to Bolingey now, turn left on reaching the road. Now comes a delightful walk up Penwartha Coombe.

"Penwartha", often spelt "Penwortha" on older maps and documents, presumably means "head of the summit" or "upper head", which seems very odd for this place; but Penwortha Farm, from which the valley takes its name, stands on higher ground. I guess the road sometimes carries a fair amount of traffic in summer, but when we last walked along it, late in 2004, all was quiet apart from the roaring stream, whose water was remarkably clear despite the torrential rains which had so recently devastated parts of Cornwall, notably Boscastle: one might have expected the run-off from fields to have made the water pretty turbid here, too. (Don't be deceived by the clarity into drinking it, however: warning signs further up the valley used to insist it is polluted.) The power in a stream like this would have been put to good use in former times. As I have mentioned on page 24, the name "Bolingey" indicates that there was a

watermill there; and soon you will reach another former mill, Nanslone, which dates back to at least 1716. ("Nans" means valley; "lone" may perhaps derive from a Celtic word meaning "grove, thicket".) The waterwheel, made at the Redruth Foundry in 1906, is still in place, and the course of the millstream which supplied it is still obvious a few feet above the road on the right side further up the valley. Bill

The waterwheel at Nanslone Mill

Trembath states that the mill was probably for "tucking" or fulling cloth. Not far beyond the mill there is a steep path up on the right; this may well have been created originally in connection with one of the small mines in this valley. When I first did this walk, back in 1994, I noticed the mouth of what I took to be a mine adit behind the low bank on the left side of the road soon after it crosses the stream; ten years later I failed to find it, but perhaps you will be more successful.

WALK 4
MINES IN AND NEAR PENWARTHA COOMBE

There were at least four: Perran Wheal Jane, otherwise called Penwortha Consols; South Wheal Leisure, otherwise Truro Consols; West Shepherds; and Lambriggan. These mines, active mainly in the mid-19th century, produced principally copper, plus a certain amount of tin, iron, silver, lead and zinc. Lambriggan was worked again in 1927-30. A.K.H. Jenkin gives an account of the slap-up dinner at Pearce's Hotel, St Agnes, that was arranged to celebrate the start of Perran Wheal Jane in 1852. "Throughout the day," he writes, "the bells rang merry peals and the evening was enlivened by performances of the St Agnes amateur brass band. Apparently the cost of these festivities proved too much for the finances of the company whose activities terminated shortly afterwards."

Continue past the Old School House, and the former school itself, dating from 1878. In its early years children from all over the parish came here: Perranporth had no school till 1898. Bill Trembath gives interesting and amusing details about the school's first headmaster and what it was like to be a pupil here.

3 Turn left immediately past the school, following the sign Public Byway. (But notice, as you do so, that the cottage almost opposite is called Mellingey, which like Bolingey means "mill-house". The present owner told us that the mill itself, a corn mill, was at the further end of the building, close to the bank which carried the leat, and the end nearer the road was the miller's cottage.) **The byway runs beside a tributary stream in another pretty valley.**

4 When you come to a footbridge, don't cross it. Here you have a choice of ways, both attractive but extremely different.

<u>A valley walk</u> (WARNING: This route is likely to be practicable only in unusually dry weather or for those well kitted-out with wellies. After the rains of late 1993 / early 1994 my wife and I gave up the attempt to get through, although in fact the flood-barrier that stopped us was probably less than 100 yards long even then. Despite this, and the mud churned up by cattle, it's worth a try, even if you do find you have to turn back, because it's such a pretty walk, mostly among trees beside the stream, which tumbles over a series of miniature rapids.) **For this route, continue ahead through the gap where there are the rotting remains of a tumbledown gate and walk beside the stream on your right - or as**

close to it as the mud allows. **Several farm gates cross or lie beside the path; just beyond the third one (not counting the slight remains beside the footbridge) is where the pools are usually deepest and the mud most glutinous. If you succeed in getting past them, keep to the track as it goes uphill between hedges. After one more gate you join a wider track and pass between a bungalow and some farm buildings. At the T-junction, where you are close to Lambourne Manor, turn left and continue along this track till it bends right and then immediately left.** (Lambourne was an important manor in medieval times, and the site of a chapel of St Edmund, but by the time Thomas Tonkin described it - about 1736 - the mansion had fallen into decay, its stones had been taken for other houses, and the chapel converted to a dwelling.) **There cross the low stone stile on your right, and you will soon be back at the church.**

<u>A walk on high ground</u> (This one was problem-free when we tried it; not pretty but offering panoramic views on a clear day.) **For this, turn left, following the signpost to the church.**

After the stony, uphill track, the path passes a high concrete stile, on the right, and then keeps to the right side of the field, passing another similar stile. The high fence prevents walkers from straying into the big field occupied, when I was last there, by the Lambriggan Deer Farm's herd of about fifty animals. (The boldest one came to greet us, as you see.) **Next you cross a lower granite stile.** At this point the view ahead includes the Carland Cross windfarm and the spoil heaps of china-clay country; looking behind, you can see St Agnes Beacon and the lonely Mithian Church on the skyline, with another windfarm, at Four Burrows, further left. **Now turn right, still keeping to the hedge on your right, and cross two more granite stiles.** Ahead now in clear conditions you can make out yet another windfarm on the skyline, the one at St Breock Downs. **Now you rejoin the path you used at the start: turn right, and continue ahead at the low stile to return to the church.**

WALK 5
HOLYWELL, ELLENGLAZE, ST PIRAN'S ORATORY & PENHALE POINT with an optional extension to CUBERT
About 8 miles (nearly 9 with Cubert)

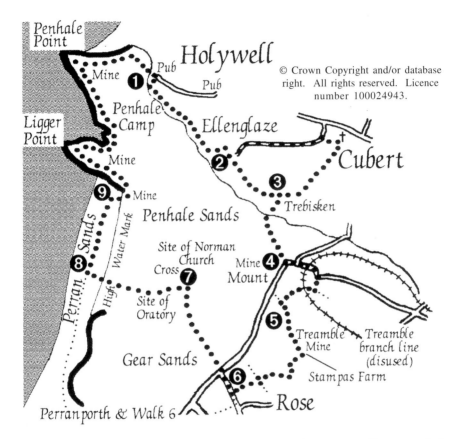

This is probably the toughest walk in the book but a very fine one. It is full of interest for the local history enthusiast and the industrial archaeologist; the big army camp at Penhale may just be a blot on the landscape for some, but for others it will add further interest. The views from Ligger and Penhale Points extend almost forty miles along the coast. The scenery is splendid and varied, including some truly awe-inspiring clifftop walking and a gentle inland section beside streams and through undulating farmland. Separating the cliffs and the farms is the strange, empty world of dunes called Gear Sands, half-hidden in which are the sites of an ancient oratory and a medieval church.

There are toilets and a choice of pubs and shops at Holywell (most if not all of them, except the pubs, closed out of season), but no other source of refreshments unless you are prepared to make the short diversion into Cubert, adding a little over half a mile to the walk. There are public toilets and shops there, but its pub recently closed.

WARNINGS: (1) The coastal path around Ligger and Penhale headlands runs close to the edge in places, and might be best avoided in rough weather and by those who suffer from vertigo - but the potentially frightening bits can easily be bypassed by taking other paths a little further inland.

(2) I do not recommend this, or Walk 6, as a walk for foggy or dusky conditions, because it would be easy to get lost among the many little paths criss-crossing the dunes, and several of the directions I give depend on your ability to see fairly distant landmarks.

Muddy conditions are likely on the inland paths. The worst section from that point of view in February 2005 was close to the Crows-an-Carn quarry (between points 4 and 5): wellies were essential! The walk includes one very steep climb, at the northern end of Perran Sands.

To drive to Holywell, take the A390 west from Truro or the B3277 south-east from St Agnes, and turn on to the A3075 Newquay road at Three Burrows (Chiverton roundabout). From Perranporth take the B3285 to Goonhavern and turn left on the main road there. Holywell is signposted on the left about three miles beyond Goonhavern. There are two quite large car parks at Holywell (one of them free to National Trust members), but both may be full at peak holiday times.

An alternative parking place is on the coast road where the walk route crosses it near point 6 on the map (grid reference SW 776553): there is room for a few cars in a layby there. This would be especially convenient for those wishing to visit the religious sites and/or the beach without necessarily doing the full round walk.

HOLYWELL

There may have been a Celtic saint called Cubert, or something similar: Catherine Rachel John believes the name is a corruption of "Gwbert", who hailed from the Cardigan area. Another theory is that the saint associated with Cubert village and Holywell is Cuthbert of Lindisfarne in Northumberland, which of all places in England is about the furthest away. The story, or legend, is that about a century after his death in 687, the monks of Lindisfarne had to flee because of Viking raids. They sailed for Ireland, taking with them the remains of St Cuthbert, but storms drove them ashore just south of Kelsey Head, where there was already a holy well. St Cuthbert's "reliques accidentally touched the well and to it communicated their qualities." Later the monks were told in a dream to return northwards; they travelled overland to Durham and laid the Saint's remains to rest in the cathedral. (Oliver Padel in "Cornish Place-Names" appears to support the case for St Cuthbert, saying that he is honoured at Gwbert in Cardiganshire too.)

No-one knows for sure which of the two "holy wells" nearby is THE holy well. The O.S. "Pathfinder" map marks the one on the beach simply as "Cave" - even that is omitted from the "Explorer" map - whereas the inland well, north of Trevornick, is labelled "Holy Well (restored)". (The restoration was carried out by Newquay Old Cornwall Society.) This one is on land owned by the Trevornick Holiday Park. The one on the beach is in a smallish cave on the north side, close to low-water mark; for fuller directions and a description, see "Around Newquay", page 66 in the second edition - also the photo on the back cover of that book.

As for Holywell itself, the trade in holidays and retirement homes has made something of a shanty-town of it, and the dominant presence of the army, based at Penhale Camp, hardly improves matters. There are compensations, though: the old, or at least "olde worlde", Treguth Inn; the strangely beautiful, ever-shifting sandhills; the splendid beach; the magnificent cliff scenery both north and south; and the fascinating evidence of mining activity around Penhale and Ligger headlands.

1 The walk starts on the path, signed Holywell Bay Holiday Park, almost opposite the St Pirans Inn; if you are coming from the NT car park it is on the right just after you have crossed the bridge beside the pub. Ignore the track on the right at the sign, "The Meadow". After passing through (or beside) the Holiday Park, follow the public footpath signs to Cubert and Ellenglaze, soon passing the Holiday Park's seasonal Costcutter store. The path runs beside the Holywell stream at first, through an area that is quite marshy in places - hence, perhaps, the name of the nearby headland, Penhale (Cornish, "head of the marsh"). This route was the official coastal footpath until the military authorities gave permission for it to skirt Penhale Camp on the seaward side; elderly acorn-signs still survive here and there.

WALK 5

The next group of houses include **Ellenglaze Manor and Farm,** and the path curves left to pass among them.

ELLENGLAZE

Ellenglaze Manor formerly comprised the whole of Cubert parish. It is mentioned in the Domesday Book, where it is called "Elil". Henderson states that "glaze", meaning "green", was added to distinguish it from the nearby manor of Elil-wyn (Helwyn or Halwyn), "the white Elil". This is mentioned again near the end of point 6 in the directions (page 47). According to a Carrick Official Guide, there is "a water wheel still in-situ behind the Manor House." A small lead-and-silver mine sank two shafts just north of Ellenglaze early in the 19th century, and its adit emptied into the marshy ground by Ellenglaze Farm - exactly where I do not know, but the disturbed area on the right of the path looks quite likely.

2 **Where the track turns left and becomes Ellenglaze Lane, you have a choice of ways:**

EITHER continue along Ellenglaze Lane in order to visit Cubert. This quiet little road runs gently uphill for about half a mile. For the quickest route to Cubert church, turn right at Churchfield Road, then left along a path which leads straight to the church via a kissing gate at the edge of the churchyard. The shops, and a fish-and-chip establishment called "Asalt & Battery", are visible from the main (north) entrance to the churchyard. Cubert's pub closed at the start of 2005, to the dismay of many villagers.

CUBERT

The original Cornish name for this village seems to have been something like Lanowyn or Lanlovey: Lanlovey Farm is nearby, and the first syllable means "church-site". (Henderson suggests that "Lanowyn" may allude to a saint called Noan, to whom three Breton churches are dedicated: Lannounan, Lannoan and Lanoan.) The later dedication of the church to "Sanctus Cubertus" (1269) or "Sanctus Cuthbertus" (1305) is discussed in the note about Holywell. Cubert's spire dates from the 14th century. Spires are not very common in Cornwall, and I suspect this one may have been added to make the tower even more prominent a landmark to guide sailors (compare St Keverne) - and perhaps also people trying to find their way across what Polsue (1867) calls the "deserts" of Cubert

Common, the Kelseys, Penhale Sands and Gear Sands. Spire and church were devastated by lightning in April 1848 but restored, "sensitively", as John Betjeman puts it, by G.E.Street in 1852. Betjeman's verdict on the church, evidently one of his favourites, is "friendly, textured, holy and humble". Sir John's "own" Cornish church of St Enodoc is another little spired church in a region dominated by dunes.

One of the oldest parts of Cubert church is a Saxon memorial stone, built into the west wall of the tower. It reads "Conetoci fili Tejernomali", translated by Arthur Mee as "Conetocius, son of Tegerno, a sad loss"; Henderson, however, takes the last word to be "Tigernomaglus". ("Tigernos" is the Brythonic word for king.) The small ancient wheel-headed cross set on a tall shaft and cemented to the wall beside the north entrance was moved here from Ellenglaze Lane in 1860. Inside the church is a 13th-century font; the old benches have gone, but some of the bench-ends were used to make the pulpit, and the chancel roof still has much of its old carved timber.

R.T.Lyon in "Cornwall's Playing Places" argues that Cubert once had its own Plain an Gwarry (see page 30), where the OS "Explorer" map marks "Settlement" about 1km from the village on the Newlyn East road. The fields on the north side were named "The Playings" on a 1696 map.

To resume the walk, leave the churchyard by the same kissing gate, then turn left immediately. Cross the estate road ahead and take the path almost opposite (slightly to the right), which runs between bungalows. At the T-junction turn right, cross the stile and make for

the right-hand edge of the field. (The right-of-way appears to cross the field diagonally, but if it is planted you may have to keep to the edge.) The path runs downhill beside the hedge and through a kissing gate, after which there are hedges on both sides. After another stile, at the bottom turn right among the buildings of Trebisken ("farmstead of the little copse or thicket", perhaps), and then left at the coast path sign. Now pick up the directions near the start of point 3: "You pass through a gate ...".

OR for the more direct route, turn right at the public footpath sign (to Trebisken). There is a wooden farm gate at this point. On the skyline to the right you can now see the stack of Mount Mine: see the later note on the Great Perran Iron Lode (page 50). After a second farm gate, go through a small wooden gate on the right, then diagonally to the right across the centre of the field, heading well to the left of the stack, and cross the stile at the field corner, which has an old coast path sign beside it. Next, go straight ahead to a gate, and through that on to a path running between two "hedges" (earth-filled stone walls which in a very short time become smothered with vegetation).

3 Just before you reach a group of buildings (Trebisken), don't miss the right turning: there is a coast path sign, but it can easily be overlooked. You pass through a gate and then walk under windswept trees beside a hedge. The footbridge is constructed partly of stout timbers which must surely once have been sleepers (cut into convenient lengths for this purpose) on the Treamble branch line. (There are notes on this - part of the Chacewater to Newquay loop - in Walks 1, 3 and 9. "Treamble" is said locally as "Tramble". The name was first recorded in 1316 as "Taranbol", "Thunderpool".) Around here the ground is marshy, but walking has been assisted by the use of more such sleepers - full-length ones here. A little way to the left, just on the far side of the stream, are the remains of Trebisken and Trebellan Mines.

TREBISKEN AND TREBELLAN MINES

These small mines produced lead and also yielded silver. Records of mining here go back to Tudor times, when a German entrepreneur called Bernard Cranach or Burchard Kranich worked a mine at "Treworthie" (Treworthen Farm is on the route of this walk) and another at Legossick in St Issey parish, between Padstow and Wadebridge. He set up a smelting house for the silver at, of all unlikely places, Lerryn, near Lostwithiel. (See "Around the River Fowey", pages 28-9 in the 2001 edition.) After two hundred years of neglect, the mines appear to have been re-started about 1786, and about ten years later were optimistically named "Wheal Mexico". The finds of silver never quite lived up to that, although Hamilton Jenkin notes that "two small parcels of the richest silver-lead ore ever raised in Cornwall" were sold by the mine in 1860. By that time the operation was working under the name Cubert United. All mining appears to have ceased in 1864.

Cross the elaborate and gradually disintegrating wooden stile, and then head just to the left of the group of dark conifers on the far side of what looks like an ancient golf-course. The path wanders a bit but is fairly clear. Cattle and farm vehicles have created something of a morass, I'm afraid, around the stile at the start and just before the gate at the end.

4 Turn left at the road. Ignore the left turning after this; continue ahead. After crossing the stream, the road passes between the piers of a former bridge carrying the Treamble line.

At Treworthen farm, where the road bends left, carry straight on along the track to the right of the farmhouse. At the next farm, North Treamble, turn right: a pretty path through an area where both mining and quarrying took place.

There are the remains of small burrows (spoil heaps) from Treamble iron mine close to the path, on the right as you go downhill (just before a more enclosed and level section which is usually very muddy underfoot). Just before you reach the stream, notice the very substantial wooden gate-post beside the path on the left. (There used to be a similar one on the right.) It marks the point where the Treamble branch line crossed. The quarry was down by the stream: the main pit, now flooded, lies beside the narrow path that cuts back sharply to the right just after you have crossed the bridge. Unfortunately the vegetation is usually too thick, at least in summer, for you to be able to see much. The quarry, which Roger Glanville believed worked until the early years of this century, was called Crows-an-Carn, meaning something like "the cross at the rock pile"; neither the cross nor the carn is evident now, so perhaps it's not surprising that the name got corrupted to "Cows and Corn", which was the name of a nearby field even when the quarry was still active. The quarry was linked to the Treamble branch by its own tramway, which was carried over the stream, supported by the two tall brick walls which still stand beside it. The main access to Treamble Mine at one time was a road or track which crossed the stream at about the same point.

5 At the T-junction turn left. Go over the bridge, through the gate, across the farmyard of Stampas Farm, and bear right. Go through the open gateway on the right (following the yellow arrow) on to a path between hedges, and turn right again, downhill, at the waymark post. This is another attractive path, but sometimes extremely muddy on both sides of the stream, although there are a few helpful - if uneven and insecure - stepping-stones. A set of water-powered Cornish stamps once worked here - hence the name of the farm you have just passed. Mr Glanville believed that the tin ore for stamping came from a mine called Wheal Thomas, a few hundred yards to the east at Hendra farm, and also probably from Mount and Rejerrah mines. No written records of Wheal Thomas seem to have survived, but it is said to have produced a little lead as well as tin, and to have ceased operations before 1830.

After the footbridge you will pass Primrose Cottage, and the drive leading up from there was indeed a mass of primroses in March. Cross two cattle-grids. Down on the left, but hidden now from view by young trees, is Rosewater fishing lake, which was excavated in about 1989. Until about a century ago, Stampas corn mill stood down there, and its millpool occupied part of what is now the lake. **At the T-junction turn right, following the sign to Gear, then left before the farm buildings at Hendravossan.** This is an interesting name, because the last part derives from the Cornish *fosyn* meaning "dykes" in the sense of walls, thus suggesting that some kind of ancient fortification or boundary wall once stood on or near its land. See also the note on Gear Sands. **The farm track curves to the right before reaching the road.**

6 Turn right, and when you reach the coast road go straight across: there is a public footpath sign. Take the most definite path, which cuts its way among gorse bushes and heads across Gear Sands towards the sea - not left, towards Perran Sands Holiday Village and Perranporth.

GEAR SANDS

The sands and nearby Gear Farm take their name from the Cornish word "ker", a round. Gear Farm is very close to Hendravossan, so both names may refer to the same ancient fortification. St Piran's Round lies only a short way south, and could be the one both farm names allude to, but Roger Glanville believed there were three such structures in close proximity. Michael Edwards (see Further Reading) describes the tank training which took place on Gear Sands during World War 2.

The white-painted concrete blocks and the old coast-path posts are very helpful on this part of the walk, where there are so few distinctive features by which to give directions. Keep watching for an ancient granite Cornish cross, over to the right (not the very tall modern concrete one, set on a ridge further left), and head for that.

Close to this are the ruins of the original Perranzabuloe parish church. (See the later note for information about the cross and the church.) A short way north-east of the cross is the openwork pit or quarry which is the most obvious relic of Halwyn iron mine. The small manor of Halwyn appears in the Domesday Book as "Elhil". The name Halwyn, common in Cornwall, normally means "white hall", but Henderson suggested a different interpretation, as mentioned in the note on Ellenglaze (page 42). Roger Glanville told me he has noticed traces of buildings and boundary hedges near the pit; whether these relate to the ancient manor, or the mine, or neither, I do not know.

7 Now head left, at first towards the tall concrete cross in the distance. (This was erected in 1969 to help people searching for St Piran's Oratory, although in fact it's quite a distance away from it. The story of its manufacture and how the 40-ton object was moved into position by means of a tank-retrieving vehicle is told by Bill Trembath.) **The path descends into a sandy hollow where in wet periods there may be a small stream. Now keep to the path heading well to the right of the concrete cross, down into another little valley, where steps lead up the side of the artificial sandhill beneath which the Oratory nestles, supposedly safe now from the elements and the vandals. Usually in the past there has been quite a deep pond in the hollow beside it; there was no sign of that early in 2005, despite lots of rain, but this little reservoir of fresh water may explain the choice of site for the Oratory.**

ST PIRAN'S ORATORY, CROSS AND CHURCH

This seems to be what happened here, so far as can be deduced from the surviving evidence:

In the late 6th century Celtic "missionaries" from Ireland, among whom was a man who has come to be known as St Piran (usually said as "Pirran", though the local pronunciation, "Pyran", seems closer to the early spelling, "Pieran"), established a monastic settlement called Lanpiran or Lamberran near a spring on this site, probably including a small "oratory" or chapel, a school, a refectory, cells for the abbot and monks and a cemetery. All the buildings are likely to have been of wattle and daub or timber. A tall granite cross (8ft 10in high) was erected at the eastern boundary. We know this was in place by 960, though possibly a little further inland than it is now. (See page 60 for more about the cross.) By that time the original oratory had been replaced by a simple stone building 29ft long and 16ft 6in wide (25ft by 12ft, according to some sources, perhaps referring to internal measurements). During the following centuries periodic flooding tended to damage the oratory, and the shifting sands always threatened to engulf it, so it seems that by about 1100 another oratory was built on higher ground near the cross, and in about 1150 the decision was taken to build a new, larger church (usually referred to now as the Norman church) on the same site. The old oratory was apparently abandoned, but never truly the "Lost Church" it has been nicknamed: the shifting sands would bury it, then reveal it again. Lanpiran or "St Piran in the Sands" (=Perranzabuloe) became an important shrine, visited by many pilgrims. The "holy relics" on show included a casket that supposedly held St Piran's head. By the 18th century even the Norman church was under threat from the sands (partly, it is said, because tinners had been allowed to divert the stream which till then had helped keep the sand back), and in 1804 work was begun on building yet another church, this time well away from the dunes at Lambourne (see Walk 4). The Norman church was finally abandoned the following year. Much of the 12th-century building was used in constructing the new one. At this time the ancient oratory was visible, but before long it seems to have been buried again. Archaeological digs took place in 1835 and 1843. A headless skeleton, one of three reportedly found under the altar in 1835, was that of an unusually tall man; tradition had it that St Piran was very tall, so the obvious conclusion was drawn - but few if any modern scholars would confidently support it. Early this century there was further excavation, and in 1910 an ugly concrete-block shelter was built around the oratory, though still allowing access for visitors and occasional services.

Damage from flooding and vandalism still occurred, and in 1980 it was decided that the only practicable way to ensure its survival was to

"Beneath this stone is buried the Oratory..."

cover it with the sands once more. The site of the Norman church was excavated in 1917-9, when the chancel walls were found to be almost complete; they, too, were safely tucked away under the dunes a few years back, but are now exposed once more. A geophysical survey of the site carried out in March 2004 suggested there are other interesting remains to be found, and the St Piran Trust and Cornwall County Council's Historic Environment Service are planning to organise a dig in September 2005 if sufficient funding can be obtained.

The story is told in more detail by Bill Trembath and especially by E.W.F. Tomlin.

Now take the wide path heading towards the sea, steering just left of the wire fence with signs warning you to keep out of the Penhale military area. Several more acorn posts show the way.

8 When you reach the beach below, even if the tide is high you should be able to walk northwards on that. (I have been told that there is in fact now a permissive path northwards among the dunes, beside or through the military area. It's not on the OS maps, but if you can find it, even at low tide you might prefer that route, because walking in the soft sand below can be tiring, and there is a hard climb back on to the cliffs at the northern end of the beach.)

At the bottom of the cliffs can be found the mouth of the adit that drained a small mine called Wheal Mary, whose buildings once stood among the dunes north-west of the Oratory. Dines (1953) called this "an old tin and copper mine", but Hamilton Jenkin, ten years later, referred to five shafts that developed two lead lodes.

There is a big variety of attractive pebbles and stones on the beach, but the further you go the more common become the rough-shaped fragments which look like bits of rusty iron - and in this case, appearances do not deceive. Just where the high cliffs start, near the end of the beach, you should be able to make out a reddish-brown streak in the rock, immediately below the point where there has been quarrying or openwork mining on the top of the cliff. Walk up to the foot of the cliff here to see the impressive caverns and shafts created by miners working this outcrop of the Great Perran Iron Lode. The mine here was called Gravel Hill. This is a place of special interest to geologists: when my late wife, Viv, and I were last there, a group of them were busy searching for traces of a rare, bright-green crystalline iron compound. (Bill Trembath mentions "rare phosphates of iron called ferro-strunzite, beraunite, and eleonirite.")

THE GREAT PERRAN IRON LODE

"The Vein has been worked formerly, and is vastly large," wrote John Woodward in about 1720. It runs inland to the south-east for at least three miles and was worked by several mines, including Gravel Hill, Halwyn, Mount (whose small stack is a prominent landmark on the inland part of this walk), Treamble and Duchy Peru (south of Rejerrah). "During the 1860s," writes Hamilton Jenkin, "the ore was drawn up the cliff from the seaward workings of Gravel Hill by a 11½ in. 'puffer' engine, whence it was carted a distance of three miles to a newly constructed quay on the Gannel for shipment." The engine house and separate stack were still substantially intact in 1937, as shown by a photograph on page 52 of H.G.Ordish's first volume. J.H.Collins describes the iron ore as "low-grade", and none of these mines, except perhaps Duchy Peru, was ever a great financial success, despite the fact that a good deal of zinc was recovered along with the haematite. The Cornwall Minerals Railway brought a line to Treamble during the 1870s, but in the event the traffic in iron ore proved a disappointment. Some open-cast iron mining was still being done at Treamble in the 1930s, and it was operated by the British Iron and Steel Corporation during the Second World War.

Gravel Hill Mine

9 Go up the very steep path just to the right of the iron lode. When the mine was working a small steam engine at the cliff-edge hauled the ore up a skip-road or tramway which occupied approximately the course of this path. **Follow the acorn signs, on up past a concrete-capped shaft and the openwork pits of Gravel Hill Mine.** The "Welcome to Penhale Sands" board gives interesting information about the area and its wildlife. As you head towards Ligger Point there is a superb view of the huge beach and past the pair of islets known as the Bawden Rocks, Cow and Calf or the Man and his Man ("man" probably deriving from the Cornish word, "maen", a stone or rock) to the cliffs as far west as Pendeen Watch (near Cape Cornwall) in very clear conditions. **The coastal footpath, marked by a series of posts, keeps near the cliff-edge and goes round Ligger Point, but if you feel insecure on any part of it there is usually at least one alternative path further inland.**

The origin of the name "Ligger" is uncertain. Padel mentions two possibilities: the Cornish language word *cleger* (cliff, crag), which gives its name to Cligga Point (Walk 7), and the dialect word *lig* (seaweed).

Soon you will see several capped, fenced-off mineshafts, relics of the Penhale Mine.

WALK 5
THE PENHALE MINE AND WHEAL GOLDEN

Four lead lodes which are also rich in silver have been found in the area round these headlands. Some copper and iron are also present. The workings go back in time well beyond existing records; by the early 19th century, three mines were operating: Penhale, at Ligger Point, Wheal Golden or Golding at Penhale Point, and East Wheal Golden, further inland. Surveys done in about 1850 revealed, writes Hamilton Jenkin, "upwards of 3,000 fathoms of drives and stopes, and 13 old men's shafts." As with so many other Cornish mines, these were shut down and re-opened according to the fluctuations of metal prices; for example, they closed in the mid-1820s; Penhale re-opened in 1830 but gave poor results; and in 1848 all three mines were amalgamated as Wheal Golden Consols.

The deepest shaft at Penhale Point began yielding copiously, and rather than transport all the ore to the Gannel and Padstow, as before, the company bought a small ship and built a landing-bay on the cliff slope on the Holywell Beach side of the headland, remains of which can still be seen (so I'm told, though I can't swear that I've found them). The whim engine was

Penhale Mine at a time when the pumping engine had been removed but the whim engine was still in place. The pumping-engine house was built for an 80-inch engine, but a 66-inch from Violet Seton Mine, Camborne, was installed. Since the "woodwork of the house" came with it, the window frames were slightly too small for the openings in the masonry, so brick infill was used around the frames, giving the house a unique appearance.

adapted for use in raising coal up the cliff face. During the winter of 1851-2, the sea broke into the Penhale Mine's workings, and the cost of repairing the breach used up all the mine's profits. In 1867, Penhale was *started up again as Penhale and Lomax, and much building was done on the Ligger headland, including that of the count-house which still remains. By 1870, the workings had reached a depth of about 800 feet and there was a workforce of 200. When the army took over the area as Penhale Camp during or shortly before the Second World War, the Penhale and Wheal Golden engine houses still dominated their headlands, but the military authorities, in Hamilton Jenkin's phrase, "wantonly demolished" them. This followed an air-raid on Penhale Camp in 1940; it was held that the old buildings were too convenient a landmark for enemy bombers. The Wheal Golden building had been particularly prominent and distinctive, and Ordish's 1934 photograph of it (page 55 in his 1967 book) shows how similar it was to the Wheal Ellen engine house in the Porthtowan valley (pages 113 and 118-9). Ordish refers to its "greenish-black clay-slate, with its bright red-brick castellated stack". The same book includes four fine 1930s photos of Penhale Mine.*

The house on the ridge above - seen more clearly from the far side of Ligger Point - was once the mine's count house. After rounding the point you have your first view of the sheer cliffs around Hoblyn's Cove, which somehow for me are made the more forbidding by the signs of all the work done on, in and under them by miners and others over the centuries. One of the great arches cut in the rock certainly looks man-made, with its unusually square top. There is an old shaft at the point where the wooden fencing on the edge of Penhale military camp begins, and later several more, two of which are right by the cliff edge.

Imagine being a miner who perhaps walked here each morning from Holywell or even from Rose -as many did - often in a howling gale, climbed down near-vertical ladders to a depth which by 1870 had reached nearly 800 feet, worked in cramped, damp and probably hot conditions for eight hours, and at last struggled up again "to grass"... Roger Glanville informed me in a letter, "Phil Penna of Hendravossan (who became President of the United Mine Workers of America) and Josiah Osborne from Rose (who became Captain of the Horn Silver Mine in Frisco, Utah) both record in their memoirs that at the age of 10 (in the late 1860s) they worked in Wheal Mary and Penhale, and went up and down these ladders attached to their fathers with a length of rope tied round their waists. They even describe the sound of the sea crashing on the shore above them."

WALK 5

The coast path runs between wooden fences beside Penhale Camp. When you reach another wooden fence encircling one of the "non-ionising radiation" masts belonging to the Royal Navy Wireless Station, look back at the sinister black cliff-face to see a couple of pieces of timber which perhaps once supported a platform and staircase leading down to the shaft entrance a few feet below; or was there formerly a horsewhim on the flattish area near the cliff edge?

The view inland includes Cubert church spire, the windmills at Carland Cross, and further left the china-clay "mountains" near St Austell.

The path continues round Penhale Point, the area mined by Wheal Golden; on the seaward side of another RN Wireless Station installation is what looks like a horsewhim plat. (See Whim in the *Some Mining Terms* section.) There is also evidence of an Iron Age cliff castle here, in the form of two banks and ditches further inland and at least one hut site.

The view along the coast that has revealed itself now stretches to the lighthouse at Trevose Head near Padstow.

Now you turn inland, towards Holywell. The path follows, at least in part, the course of the mine tramway which served the landing-bay mentioned earlier. What looks like a concrete shaft-cap with iron hoops at the cliff edge is in fact used by the Army for rock-climbing and abseiling exercises.

As you reach Holywell, the St Pirans Inn is just by the path, and a little way up the road is the Treguth Inn, which occupies an old farmhouse, claimed to date from the 13th century. John N. Rosewarne's selection of old photographs, *Bygone Cornwall*, published by D. Bradford Barton in 1970, includes one of Treguth Farm in the days before the motor-car invaded Cornwall, when the farmer's cows "were able to seek shade and coolness on the beach." Even at that time, though, "real Cornish teas" were served at the farmhouse. Its name probably means "farm of the hollow or enclosure".

WALK 6

PERRANPORTH, PERRAN SANDS, ST PIRAN'S ORATORY
& ROSE with an optional visit to ST PIRAN'S ROUND

About 4½ miles, or 5 with the diversion

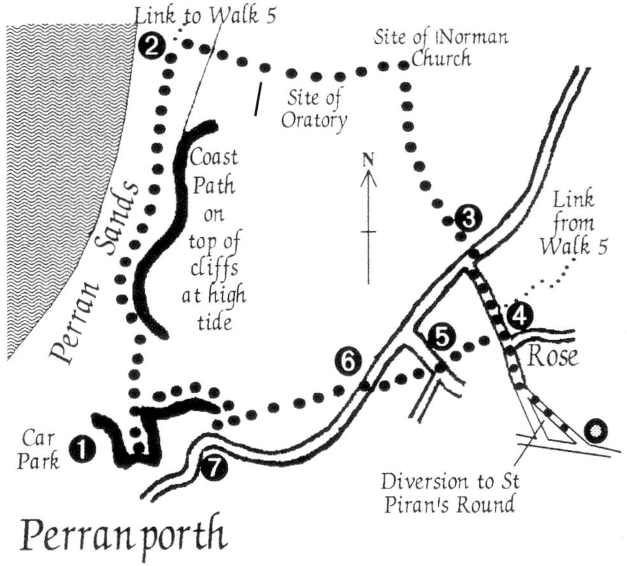

Link to Walk 5

❷

Site of Norman Church

Site of Oratory

Coast Path on top of cliffs at high tide

Perran Sands

N

❸

Link from Walk 5

❺ ❹

❻

Rose

Car Park ❶

❼

Diversion to St Piran's Round

Perranporth

If you can, start this walk when the tide is fairly low and still on the way out; otherwise you will be unable to inspect some interesting caves, many of which bear evidence of mining activity. It would be helpful to bring a torch if you want to look for that. At high tide you will have to walk on the cliffs rather than the beach. The suggested route repeats, in the opposite direction, the path across Gear Sands, visiting the site of St Piran's Oratory and the ruins of the medieval church of St Piran, which are included in Walk 5.

I do not recommend this, or Walk 5, as a walk for foggy or dusky conditions, because it would be easy to get lost among the many little paths criss-crossing the dunes, and several of the directions I give depend on your ability to see fairly distant landmarks.

It is quite an easy walk, except that Perran Sands can be a little too soft for comfort, and there is a fairly steep climb up the sandhills when you turn inland, if you have come along the beach. Perranporth has toilets, shops and pubs, a folk museum and an information centre. (See Walk 7.)

Directions for driving to Perranporth are given for Walk 7. This walk, too, starts at the main car park.

WALK 6
PERRANPORTH & ST PIRAN

Perranporth and the parish of Perranzabuloe (Latin, "in sabulo": in the sand) take their name from the 6th-century saint Piran, who arrived in this part of Cornwall from Ireland rather unconventionally, floating on a millstone to which he had been tied by heathens before being thrown over a cliff into a stormy sea. (Those of a down-to-earth disposition may prefer the theory that the "millstone" was actually a small altar of the sort that many such early saints are said to have taken around with them.) Several other places in the county are dedicated to him, notably a chapel at Tintagel, the church at Perranuthnoe in the west, and the inland parish of Perranarworthal south-west of Truro. He is the patron saint of the tinners, having been credited with the discovery of tin, or with teaching the miners the art of smelting. The Cornish flag or banner, St Piran's Cross, is said to represent "the light of the gospel shining in a world of sin" and to depict the cross he made from molten white tin. St Piran's Day (5th March) is celebrated throughout Cornwall each year, and since 2000 a "pilgrimage" to St Piran's Cross on Gear Sands has taken place on the following Sunday. A bronze statue of the saint by Peter Walker is due to be erected in 2006 "at the spot where he came ashore".

Since for centuries it was mining alone - apart from pilchard seining - that supported the population of Perranporth, its patron saint is a fitting one. Tin was produced, but also lead, silver, zinc and especially copper. "Miles of galleries lie beneath the village," writes Bill Trembath, who gives a vivid account of what the place must have looked, sounded and smelt like when the two principal mines - Great Wheal Leisure in the centre and to the east, Perran Great St George to the west - were active. The drawing below, based on one of the earliest Cornish photographs (probably about 1850), shows (to the left and in the foreground) the two

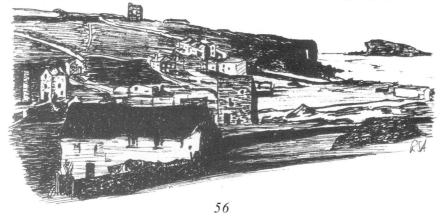

engine houses of Wheal Leisure, already ruined by about 1850. They originally contained pumping engines with 70- and 66-inch cylinders. Between 1827 and 1840, this mine sold nearly 52,000 tons of copper ore. Both mines closed early in the 1870s, after years of bitter territorial disputes, but there is valuable metal still to be had in these rocks. Michael Edwards (see Further Reading) tells of the collapse of an old shaft belonging to Wheal Leisure in the late 1930s. (See the photos on pages 108-9 in L.J.Bullen's Volume 5 - the same shaft, I presume.) The shaft was then "temporarily capped" and gravelled over, and in the run-up to D-Day US army officers used it and the surrounding area for parking. The cap gave way - and it is said there's a jeep down there still!

Not long after the demise of the mines, the great shoals of pilchards suddenly deserted the Cornish coasts.

Although the holiday trade as we understand it began in earnest here only after the arrival of the railway in 1903, Perranporth had been a favourite day-trip destination for Truronians a century earlier. By the latter part of the 19th century sea-bathing at Perranporth was sufficiently popular for segregation of the sexes to be deemed necessary on the western beach: gentlemen bathers only till 9 am, ladies only from 9 till midday!

1 Go over the bridge on the right (as you look out to sea) side of the car park. Cross the second bridge and head north towards the distant headland, Ligger Point, which marks the end of the two-mile stretch of Perran Sands. On your right you will see how the sand-dunes have, mainly since the early 1980s, been planted with marram grass to stabilise them; without that they are nearly as mobile as the sea, and much evidence of the miners' activities in these parts is now buried under the sand.

Having passed "The Watering Hole" and the Perranporth Surf Life Saving Club's HQ, you will reach an outcrop of cliffs (Cotty's Point, known locally at Flat Rocks) and if the tide is against you you will have to climb the path to the top of these, following the acorn signs. It is rather hard work, with its many climbs and descents, but it rewards you with an interesting information board, "Welcome to Penhale Sands", at the start and with good views as you walk on. About 50 yards along from the board, a wooden hut used to stand on the left side of the path; here Winston Graham would come to find the peace and quiet - and perhaps also the inspiration - he needed to write his books. (See the note about Perran Consols.) The Perranzabuloe Museum Trust is currently gathering funds in order to place a commemorative bench on the site; the hope is that it will be in place by the end of 2006. **(For some guidance with the clifftop route, see the last paragraph on page 59.)**

(For some guidance with the clifftop route, see the last paragraph on page 59.)

Even if you do go that way, you may be able to look into one or two of the caves first, and work out which if any of these holes are mine adits. The little one on the right of the steps is certainly man-made, for example, and the first sizeable cave to the left contains the mouths of two adits, one of which is on the right soon after you enter. The small cave after that seems to have a narrow drainage shaft in the roof ... and so on: if you have the time to explore them all, and especially if you brought a torch, there are plenty of opportunities for detective work - and even those not yet bitten by the "industrial archaeology" bug will have to agree that many of the larger caves are impressive enough to be worth a look. Some display beautiful, glistening rock-strata and amazingly vivid stains caused by the minerals in the dripping water, and the force of the tide is shown not only by the stacks of driftwood at the far ends of deep caves, but also by the bits of debris lodged high up in side-clefts. The holes, usually square-sided, a few feet up the cliff-face are almost certainly adits, set above high-tide mark. Near the end of the stretch of high cliffs is an adit mouth (Wheal Byan Adit) at beach level with a steady flow of water issuing from it.

These workings were parts of several small mines; the closest to Perranporth were Wheal Ramoth (pronounced "Raymoth") and North Leisure, and most of the others were grouped under the name of Perran Consols.

PERRAN CONSOLS

There were at least six ancient mines here: Wheal Creeg, Wheal Vlow (pronounced to rhyme with "how"), Wheal Widden, Wheal Mary, Wheal Hope, Rose Mine and Budnick; Vlow was "worked for tin before 1750" according to J.H.Collins, and records of Creeg go back to 1774. Their main shafts and buildings were about half a mile inland. From 1835 to 1840 they were amalgamated as Perran Consolidated and employed a hundred people. The title was revived in the 1870s, when Wheal Vlow's shafts were taken down to 240 feet below the level of the adit, and this mine was prospected again in 1927, but without success. Wheal Mary lay a little further north than the route of this walk.

In Winston Graham's "Poldark" novels, the mine Ross owned at the end of the 18th century could well have been based on one of this group. Bill Trembath says Wheal Vlow was his model, but that he confused matters by naming the fictional mine after another one nearby, Wheal Leisure. Incidentally, the name "Nampara", also made famous by "Poldark", is that of a group of cottages near St Michael's Church in Perranporth; locals pronounce it "Namperra".

The lower cliffs that follow show much less, if any, evidence of mining; then follows a large area of dunes. The pebbles on the beach are exceptionally attractive, and their very varied colouring hints at the complexity of the rock formations nearby.

I recommend Bill Trembath's account of the walk along Perran Sands (pages 87-9): the details he provides about the locality and its wildlife would, I think, add greatly to your enjoyment of this section.

Directions for those who have walked along the beach continue at point 2 below.

THE CLIFFTOP ROUTE: After an acorn sign, follow the downhill path to join the tarmac road which runs down from the caravan / camping park. Perran Sands holiday centre, which recently added new shops and a Burger King to its amenities, covers 550 acres and attracts up to 5,000 visitors per week during the summer. It employs a ranger, whose duties include protection of the dunes and their flora and fauna. **Where the road curves right, after about 100 yards, the coast path is clearly signed ahead. At the big, open, grassy area, head up towards the mobile homes to find another acorn sign beside a row of what look like short lengths of telegraph pole. Now follow the acorn signs till you reach a fairly deep, sandy valley. This is where you turn inland to find the sites of the Oratory and medieval church. The path is very clear at first but soon becomes less so. A little way to the left is a long fence with "Keep Out" signs (the boundary of the military area); keep**

fairly close to that. **Now skip the next paragraph and pick up the directions at "Soon you will see..."**

2 To find St Piran's Oratory, you need to climb the sandy slope near the far end of the area of dunes just mentioned - that is, just before a few more rocky outcrops show through, and keeping to the right of the signs warning you to stay clear of the military area. Continue ahead, always keeping the warning signs close on your left.

Soon you will see ahead a tall concrete cross, set on one of the highest ridges. It is intended to guide people to the Oratory, although in fact it is not very close to it. (Bill Trembath tells how the cross was made by a local builder in his own garden and set in place in 1969 by a tank-retrieving vehicle which had to be brought by road from north-east England.) **The sandy hillock under which the Oratory is buried is about a couple of hundred yards further north (left as you approach on this walk), at a lower level and quite close to the military area fence; an inscribed granite slab (photo, page 49) at the top of a short flight of steps marks the spot. I hope you'll find it!**

From there, a well-trodden path leads further inland to the ruins of the Norman church of St Piran. Standing beside them is an ancient cross which in clear conditions can be seen on the skyline. A few yards beyond the cross, the public footpath turns right (south) and continues across Gear Sands to meet the coast road at a kissing-gate. The course of the path is made clear by a series of wooden posts bearing black or white acorn symbols, and also many white-painted concrete blocks. All this part of the route is described in reverse direction in Walk 5, which has notes on the Oratory, the church and Gear Sands.

Only one other Cornish cross - at Egloshayle, Wadebridge - has three holes right through the head. The wind-driven sand in this area may explain the fact that there is little decorative carving on the cross.

3 (If you want to get back to Perranporth by the most direct route, you could turn right and follow the coast road till you reach the path on the right at point 6. Even out of season, however, this road, and especially the B3285, which it soon joins, can be quite busy, so I would recommend the following route, keeping to minor roads and paths.) **Cross the coast road and continue almost straight ahead along the minor road into Rose village.**

ROSE

To trot out the oft-repeated remark about the Roseland, this name has nothing to do with flowers, but probably derives from the Cornish "ros", moorland. The interesting article about Rose in the WI's "Cornwall Village Book", however, mentions two rival explanations. One relates to the local belief that the original settlement was closer to the sea and was engulfed by the ever-shifting sands, like St Piran's Oratory and the mythical city of Langona or Langarrow. (See the note on Cubert Common in "Around Newquay".) The story goes that the surviving villagers moved inland and built a new village, calling it "Rose" because it rose from the sand. The other explanation is that the name derives from a Celtic word meaning circle or wheel, referring to St Piran's Round. The same article describes Rose when the local mines were active: "it had four shops, two pubs, a bakery and a shoemaker, and a population of about 1,400." The disappearance of shops is in fact a much more recent event than the demise of the mines: people living there now tell me it's not long since there were three. (A tiny post office, which opened only twice a week, was the last survivor.) Roger and Maureen Glanville's 195-page book, "Rose, The Story of a Village and its People, The Rosillians" was published in 2004, two years after Roger's death. It can be obtained from local bookshops or by phoning Mrs Glanville on 01872-572784.

4 Just past the telephone kiosk take the public footpath on the right.
    (But if you would like to include a visit to St Piran's Round, a short diversion at this point - about a quarter of a mile each way - will bring you to it. For that, continue ahead, past the chapel. The original chapel was in fact the building on the right, now converted into a private house, and the present chapel started life as the Sunday School, at a time when there were 120 pupils! This gives some measure of the extent to which the village population has declined since the heyday of mining in this locality. **Go on past the left turning to Lower Rose, and immediately**

beyond the bungalow named "The Smithy" fork left on to a byway that leads straight to the Round. See pages 30-31 for information about it. Return the same way, taking the footpath on the left just before the phone box.)

After the gate, keep as close to the left edge of the field as the churned-up mud allows, then go through the kissing-gate and up a few steps at the field corner. Near the end of the field, there are shafts in the gorse-patch on the left. These are Bice's Shafts, part of Budnick Mine (see page 31 again). On the right of the path at the top of the steps is the former site of the mine's dressing floors (now overgrown).

5 At the road, turn right, ignore the left turning and cross the stile with a metal bar over it at the corner. Next cross the wooden stile on the right (avoiding crossing what is now a football pitch); the path now heads across another field to a tall Public Footpath sign beside a low granite stile.

6 Cross the road with care and continue in exactly the same line, heading for Perranporth across the golf course, following the line of white-painted stones. (These are few and far between in places, but the path runs dead-straight according to the OS maps.) Eventually the path joins a little tarmacked road; go on down it for a few yards, then take the flight of steps down to the left. A sandy path brings you to the main road.

7 Turn right and almost immediately right again; follow the Ponsmere ("Great Bridge") River round to the two bridges and the car park. The river used to spread out wide as it ran across the beach; to reduce this problem and enable it to be bridged it was diverted into its present channel.

WALK 7
PERRANPORTH, PERRANCOOMBE, MITHIAN, TREVELLAS COOMBE AND THE COAST
About 7½ miles

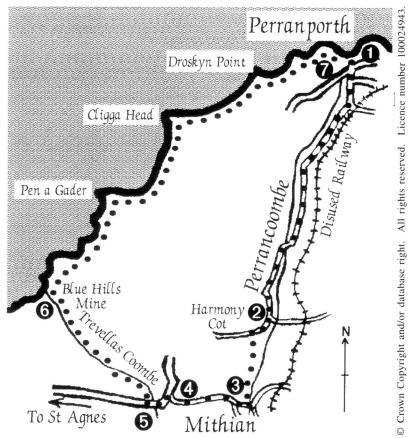

Another very fine walk, beginning this time inland, mostly by valley streams. The coastal section is particularly dramatic. It starts with an extremely steep climb but after that is fairly level. Plan the walk, if possible, so that the tide is low when you get back to Perranporth; you can then explore the area of ancient mining in the cliffs at the west end of the beach. No-one staying in this area should miss Trevellas Coombe. Most of the inland walking is on roads, but these are usually quiet apart from one short stretch. The path following point 2 on the map is often muddy. A pleasant pub, the Miners Arms, is very conveniently placed at Mithian.

63

The walk begins at the main car park in Perranporth, overlooking the beach. To drive there from St Agnes, take the B3285 eastwards; from Truro, take the A390 westwards to Chiverton Cross roundabout, turn right on to the A3075 (Newquay) road, turning left for Perranporth where signposted.

See pages 56-7 for a note about Perranporth.

1 We start with the inland section of the route, so walk back past the Tywarnhayle pub, cross the bridge (at the road junction) and go along Boscawen Road, passing Lloyds TSB on your left, and the lake in Boscawen Gardens and later St Michael's Church on your right. Built in 1872 as a "chapel of ease" (the parish church is far away at Lambourne), this pretty and well-cared-for church has at the east end a window dedicated to Donald Healey, the famous rally driver and designer of sports cars (1898-1988), who was born in Perranporth. **Where the road becomes Perrancoombe, notice the remains of the railway bridge at the corner, part of the Chacewater to Newquay loop line, described in notes on other walks. A pleasant short path has been created along the top of the embankment, so I suggest you go up the steps and continue as far as possible, then return to the valley road and turn left.**

Immediately after passing a large pine tree beside the road on the right, look down close to the road on that side and you will see a buddle, probably nearly full of water and/or fallen leaves, and a few fragments of ruined buildings. These are probably relics of Perran Coombe Stamps; two photos of this small operation at work in 1924 are in Bullen, Vol.5.

Where the main road curves left, keep straight on, signed to Leycroft. After the bridge over the stream and the nearby pump, the valley becomes more rural and much more attractive. This is Carnbargus (which seems to mean "the rock-pile of the kite"). A little further on, disturbed ground on the right and at least one Clwyd-capped shaft on the left are relics of a small mine called Prince Royal. It was also, at various times, called Princess Royal and Prince Albert Consols; unfortunately, these expressions of loyalty to the monarchy don't seem to have been rewarded by much commercial success. Soon you enter the district called Blowinghouse, referring to the early type of tin-smelting works which employed a bellows, usually powered by a waterwheel, to raise the furnace temperature. Blowinghouse Mill appears to have been served by a leat on the right, carried across the road by a launder.

2 **Where you join another road, near a ford, keep straight on. To continue the walk, turn left a few yards later on to a path which begins at a rough stile on the left of a pair of metal gates; but first it's worth walking about a hundred yards further along the road to see the attractive thatched cottage called Harmony Cot, birthplace of John Opie.**

JOHN OPIE

Born in 1761, the son of a mine carpenter-cum-builder, John or "Jan" Opie was a multi-talented man, a mathematician and philosopher who earned the nickname "little Sir Isaac", but it was as a portrait painter that he achieved fame and a second nickname, "The Cornish Wonder". John Wolcot, a Truro doctor and satirical writer better known by his pseudonym Peter Pindar, "discovered" Opie, gave help and encouragement, and in 1781 took him to London, introducing him to the people who mattered in the art world. He exhibited 143 pictures at the Royal Academy in London, and produced in all about 750 paintings as well as many illustrations, especially of Shakespeare. He died aged only 45, poisoned, some said, by the lead in his paints. After a lavish funeral, in which his hearse, drawn by six black horses, was followed by 59 other coaches of mourners, he was buried in the crypt of St Paul's Cathedral.

The St Agnes Museum has a John Opie display including a self-portrait. In the Royal Cornwall Museum at Truro is an interesting example of his work, entitled "Gentleman and a Miner". Painted in 1786, it is a portrait of Thomas Daniell, the father of "Guinea-a-Minute Daniell": see the notes on Wheal Towan in Walk 10 (page 113) and on the Mansion House (Truro) in Volumes 1 and 3 of "A History of Truro", published by Landfall.

The Opies' cottage was called "The Blowing House" until John's first wife, Mary, made him change it. A stream which could have been harnessed for the waterwheel runs close to the cottage. Prettier the new name may have been, but it must have developed ironic overtones in the following years, during which he neglected her until finally she ran off with a Major. By 1874 the name had been changed again, to "Woodcocks"; when it reverted to "Harmony Cot" I don't know.

From Harmony Cot return to the Mithian footpath, going through the small kissing-gate on the right as soon as you have crossed the stile by the big gates. A series of yellow waymarkers on wooden posts show the way at first. Later you cross a pair of stiles, and the path

continues close to the stream. After another stile (in urgent need of repair in April 2005), a few steps take you up into a wooded stretch, and soon you will reach a small group of ruined buildings, securely fenced around. These are the remains of a cottage and the site of an old grist mill, Magor's Mill. A photograph in Clive Benney's 1850-1920 volume and in Tony Mansell's *Mithian* shows Mithian Old Mill as it was in about 1906.

Among the trees on the far side of the valley, as you approach the road, is the imposing Georgian manor house called Rose-in-Vale, now a hotel and restaurant but formerly the home of Captain John Oates, who had a controlling interest in many local mines including Wheal Leisure at Perranporth, and made a fortune from the Navvy Pit. (See the note on Wheal Music on pages 107-8.)

3 At the road turn right into Mithian. At the Miners Arms, turn right and continue up the road. The Round House, on the left, was probably originally Mithian Farm's "whim house" for grinding corn: a horse or donkey would walk round and round inside to turn the top millstone.

MITHIAN

The name, as Padel says, looks Cornish, but its origin and meaning are unknown. A settlement called "Mithien" appears in a document dated 1201, and the Miners Arms is old, but just how old is in doubt: one of its plaster ceilings has been thought to bear the date 1577, but Tony Mansell reads it as 1775. The pub also has its "secret passage", linking it to the manor house opposite (now converted into five small dwellings) - or rather it used to have, since much of the tunnel has now collapsed. Some say it was a "priest hole" and that in Tudor times the local squire was executed for sheltering Roman Catholic priests. (Compare the story of Golden Manor, page 124 in "From the Roseland to St Austell Bay".) The pub is "famed for its ghost" according to Colin Gregory, reporting in the "West Briton" (17 March 2005). Various strange happenings, such as chairs being thrown about in apparently empty rooms, had led the landlady to write to the Diocese of Truro for help in "putting to rest a spirit which was frightening people", and only two days later a fire broke out, causing damage mainly to the roof. Was this a warning from the world of the supernatural?

Mithian Church was built in 1860-1; the original tower and spire were demolished as unsafe in 1898 and not replaced till 30 years later, when a new tower, without spire, was built of stone taken from an old engine house. Please don't waste your time searching Mithian for the church: it's three miles away, near the Chiverton Cross roundabout. Mithian's tiny post office is also quite a way from the village centre (at or near Barkla Shop). "Mithian," says the WI's "Cornwall Village Book", "once boasted a bakery, a tailor, a shoemaker, three shops ... (and) ... a Methodist chapel"; now they exist only in the memory, like the mines which provided employment, and Mithian Halt, on the railway line that closed in 1963. Wheal Prosper to the north and Wheals Mithian, Liberty, Valley and Frederick to the south were the closest mines, but they had finished by around the middle of the 19th century. Mansell mentions other small mines of which little if any trace remains, at least above ground.

4 Turn left at the T-junction. Please take care on this busy road; it's best to stay on the left side till you have rounded the right bend. **Continue down to Barkla Shop, the small group of houses where the stream flowing down Trevellas Coombe crosses the road.** "Shop" refers to a smithy, probably named after the original blacksmith. By about 1900 it was Alf Crebo's smithy, and a wheelwright's shop was next door; photographs of both are on page 69 of Clive Benney's 1996 book.

5 Turn right on to the path just past the bridge - a pretty, wooded walk by the stream. When you come to a wider track, bear right. In the area just behind you at this point - that is, in the triangle formed by the road, the path you came on and the wider track - was Jericho Stamps.

JERICHO STAMPS

West Kitty mined the tin beneath St Agnes village and could not set up dressing floors there, so all the ore had to be transported by horse-and-cart to Trevellas Coombe. The cost of the two-mile haul eventually contributed to the mine's downfall. In this quiet spot now it is hard to imagine the activity, grime and racket which must have surrounded the quite large industrial complex shown in my drawing, which is based on an undated postcard. Half-hidden among the trees and undergrowth are the remains of many buildings, some of them quite substantial; now that nature has taken over again so completely, it seems amazing that Jericho Stamps was still a going concern well into the 20th century. J.A.Buckley's "Cornish Mining - at Surface" has an amazing photograph of it, dating from around 1900. The still substantial ruins on the site in 1925 are

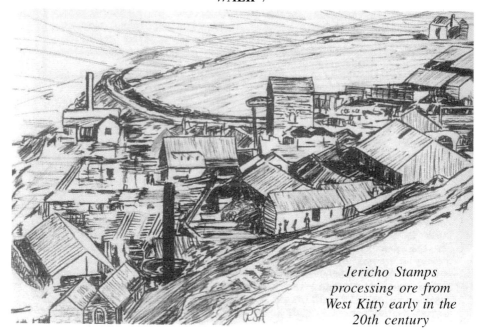

Jericho Stamps processing ore from West Kitty early in the 20th century

shown in a photograph in Clive Benney's later volume. ("One cylinder bolt of the stamps engine is still visible!" Kenneth Brown tells me.) I have not come across an explanation of "Jericho"(sometimes spelt "Jerico"), but many Cornish places were given Biblical names in the time of men like Billy Bray, the miner-evangelist from Twelveheads, near Bissoe: Bethel and Salem are two other examples, and "Promised Land" is about a mile from here. Trevellas Coombe is commonly known as Jericho Valley.

Cross the footbridge, then keep left near the stream, passing beside Jericho Cottage, which was built on or close to the site of a burning house. Soon after this, if you look to your right you will find the portal of an adit, now bricked up. As the valley opens out towards the sea, evidence of tin streaming, as well as lode mining, grows more and more obvious.

BLUE HILLS TIN STREAMS
To give you an idea of how much has changed here in recent years, here is how I described this area back in 1989. The photo dates from then.
"On the left just before you reach the fishponds are the remains of a twelve-headed stamps machine, once driven by a waterwheel:

the leat is still there. Six of the stamps' "lifters" remain, and on the big axle can be seen the cams which raised them and let them drop on the ore. Also visible are the ratchet teeth to stop them running backwards and being damaged. A few yards further on, a dismantled

waterwheel is propped against the wall beneath the track. This was brought from Penzance about 1984 or 1985. Tin streaming and smelting are still carried out by members of the Wills family in this part of Trevellas Coombe, although while tin prices remain low the family also need other occupations such as fish farming."

The fish farming is no longer needed now, because Colin and Mark Wills have created a thriving little enterprise, by which the whole process of tin streaming is carried out, from the stamping of the ore to the production of articles made of tin. In addition to the restored stamps

(this photo shows the restoration under way in 1995), the buddle is now in working order, as are a small ball-mill, shaking table and smelter. The clear and colourful explanations and demonstrations given by both father and son make visits very worthwhile. Tours, which last about an hour and a half, normally take place between 10.30 and 5, April to October. Blue Hills Tin Streams can be contacted by phone on 01872 553341.

Colin tells the story of tin streaming in Trevellas Coombe in the Journal of the St Agnes Museum Trust, No. 15.

Lower down the valley, you will see the entrance of a level shaft beside the engine house; it has been blocked off after about 30 feet. The ruined mine buildings (several of which have recently been repointed by Carrick District Council), the burrows and the shafts are relics of Blue Hills Mine.

Blue Hills Mine

Right: The
pumping-engine
house and stack
as they look now
Below: *from a*
photo taken
about 1890

Pumping-engine house

Stack
(now
shortened)

Flywheel of
stamps/whim
engine

BLUE HILLS MINE

This tin mine was active, although not working continuously, between 1813 and 1898, but there were many smaller workings here at least as far back as the 18th century, and there are records of stamping mills in the valley in 1693. The lodes being worked were mined by Goonlaze and Penhalls Mines and Wheal Kitty a little further west, and they are all linked underground. The engine house was built for a 70-inch pumping engine; the shaft beside its bob wall has been filled in, but the balance-bob pit is still visible. (See "Exploring Cornish Mines" Vol. 1 and the Cornwall Archaeological Unit's study for more detail.)

When you reach the road, bear right, and follow the coast path sign. The lower track gives you the better view of the stack and the pit near it. The pit was constructed for the flywheel of a horizontal whim and stamps engine. Near the edge of the low cliff are yet more mine buildings. If you care to scramble down to the beach you will be able to look more closely at the mouth of an adit, where water is flowing out quite near the notice warning of dangerous currents.

6 Now you have a stiff climb up the hillside on the right, following the coastal footpath back to Perranporth. Take the middle one of the three footpaths, on which a few wooden steps have been provided. (Rather more of them are needed, I think, especially for walkers descending the slope in wet weather.) **Having (eventually!) reached the top, keep to the main path, which soon heads a little inland - although you could walk round the headland if you wish.** Now you are faced by spectacular red cliffs, whose contorted strata give some idea of the mineral richness of the land hereabouts. The green stains, very bright on some of the cliffs between here and Perranporth, are evidence of copper.

Next the path runs through part of a World War 2 airfield, created in 1940-1 and used mainly by Spitfire squadrons. The twelve odd-looking bunkers, named by Robert Andrew (see Further Reading) as "double blast pens", were constructed, he says, to protect the aircraft from enemy attack as well as from the weather. One Wing Commander quoted in his book states, "At Perranporth the winds were so strong that the Spitfires had to be tied down by means of large corkscrew pieces of metal driven into the ground and rope hawsers to wings and tail." RAF Portreath closed in 1945. Trevellas Airfield, as the part still in use for aviation is now known, has been used since the late 1950s mainly by a gliding club. It has been the focus of much controversy in recent years because of plans by its owners to increase greatly the number of aircraft using it.

Soon after this, just past Pen a Gader ("headland of the chair or seat"), there are shafts near the cliff-edge, and a hole near the foot of the cliff looks like an adit; these are probably workings of Wheal Prudence.

WHEAL PRUDENCE

"A very ancient mine," says Collins. Recorded sales of copper go back to 1812, but some of the adits whose mouths are scattered everywhere on the hillsides and cliff-faces on this stretch of coast are much older than that, and Prudence was really a group of older mines with such names as Hanover Cove, Wheal Jacka, Wheal Cock and Wheal Meadow. About 1826, Prudence was bought by a London company and amalgamated with Cligga and Great St George mines; this enterprise closed in 1839,

but in 1862 a house for a 70-inch pumping engine was erected and a new shaft sunk, about 100 yards inland, to a depth of about 700 feet. (To help you imagine that: the mine's adit, issuing at the bottom of the cliff, was 300 feet "below grass".) " 'The failure of the last working,' explained the Mining Journal 15th November 1862, 'was due to the unjudicious attempt to work the sea-ward lodes by direct workings from a detached and storm-beaten island rock instead of by a cross-cut.' On this prominence was sunk the Island Shaft which can only be approached today by a crumbling knife-edged path, bordered on one side by the awe-inspiring chasm of the 'Old Prison' and on the other by the scarcely less sheer cliffs of Cocking's Cove." (A.K.H.Jenkin: "Mines and Miners of Cornwall") The miners reached the island by means of a wooden bridge, the site of which can still be seen. In February 1863 the Mining Journal reported that "the resident agent...and the engineers...have displayed much energy in getting such an amount of work done in the winter months in such a situation...exposed to the full sweep of the Atlantic so that during the north-westerly gales spray from the waves frequently flew over the engine-house, driving the workmen from their posts." In the following years, however, the costs involved in undersea mining proved a problem, and the mine closed in 1868. Collins mentions "sales of small quantities of black tin and copper ore up to 1879". The 70-inch engine house was blown up during World War 2, for the same reason as those at Penhale Mine and Wheal Golden (see the note on pages 52-3); the base of the house and the shaft can still be seen.

The main headland in front now is Cligga Head (Cornish "cleger": rocks, cliff). Notice the adits in the cliff below it. Soon the path passes through a big area where it seems the miners have left hardly a stone unturned. There are shafts very close to the cliff-edge in the section where the indentations are particularly dramatic.

CLIGGA HEAD

The Cligga area has been mined for tin for centuries. Several groups of ruined concrete buildings give evidence of quite recent industry: some date from World War 2, when wolfram was mined here, others from the early 1960s, when Geevor Tin Mines Ltd sank a 200-foot shaft, and yet others may have been erected in the '70s, when further prospecting was done. The concrete buddles and other remains of dressing floors on the headland itself are of 1930s and/or World War 2 vintage.

Just to the east of the headland there was a dynamite works, founded in 1889 as the British and Colonial Explosives Company and taken over in 1893 by the Nobel Explosives Company of Peace-Prize fame. It ceased manufacturing explosives in 1905 but was revived during World War I. At that time nearly a thousand people were employed, but the works closed almost as soon as hostilities ended. Details of the history and layout of the explosives works are given in Bryan Earl's "Cornish Explosives" (Trevithick Society, 1978), which includes a large-scale map and photographs. Bill Trembath tells of the watchman who guarded the nitroglycerine nitrator plant: his stool, it is said, had only one leg, so that if he should nod off he would have a rude and speedy awakening!

After Cligga, the coastal footpath continues a little lower, near the cliff-edge. (There is also a path at a higher level - unofficial but clearly well-walked - and you may prefer that if you find this section of the coast path unnerving. It is certainly safer in wet or windy conditions.) Now you are in the area worked by Great St George (otherwise known as Good Fortune), Wheal Perran, Wheal Leisure and Droskyn mines. Quite soon on your right if you are on the coast path, don't miss the entrance to an adit, one of the best examples in the area; it is easily accessible and can be explored if you have a torch - but please take great care. As you approach the headland at the west side of Perranporth beach (Droskyn Point), notice what Barry Atkinson calls "a particularly awesome man-made cavern, with passages leading off from it"; a fairly easy path leads down to it. **Continuing on the coastal footpath, eventually you will reach a kissing-gate by a road.**

7 Continue downhill, and turn left past the front of the "Droskyn Castle" former hotel (now apartments).

If the tide is high, return to the car park via the signed coast path below road level, which passes Perranporth's attractive Millennium sundial and eventually rejoins the road. Notice as you go the "caves" and arches in the small headland, most of which are in fact the work of countless miners over the centuries. Further out is Chapel Rock, named, it is said, from an ancient small chapel, probably the home of a hermit, whose foundations were still visible in 1922 but have now been swept away by the sea, along with much of the rock itself.

At low tide, however, it is well worth going round to the left and down steps to the rocks below. A fair bit of scrambling is involved, but

Miners as well as the elements have played their part in shaping the cliffs at Perranporth.

for those interested in the ancient mines it is worth the effort. There are innumerable adit-mouths, some a few feet up the cliff, and the whole headland is obviously honeycombed with shafts. Some man-made arches remain, others have collapsed, and the original shape of the cliffs has been entirely altered, as shown by the drawing on page 56, based on a photograph taken about 1850. Hamilton Jenkin writes: "In some places...workings were continued downward by means of shafts to a depth of 10 or 15 fathoms below sea level. To drain these, water was brought by a leat two miles up the Perran Coombe stream and thence through a tunnel, 700 ft. long, which was driven beneath the upper portion of the cliffs near the present Tywarnhayle Road." (Bill Trembath gives some details about the water channel, known as "Susan Tregay's Droke".) "From here," continues Jenkin, "the water descended through the most easterly shaft of the Old Droskyn Mine where it passed over a 22ft. diameter pumping-wheel which was housed in an underground chamber hewn out of the solid rock. Beyond that the water flowed through a further tunnel, and over launders suspended across a cave, to another shaft, some 280 ft. to the west, where it drove another wheel of similar dimensions."

It is only at exceptionally extreme spring tides that at low water you can walk round the small headland to the west and visit the magnificent caves known as Cathedral Caverns. Their old name was Vugah-en-Plunder, a hint of their value to smugglers or perhaps wreckers; it was, says Mr Trembath, the first Bishop of Truro who coined the more respectable name. Some dramatic mine workings are visible there, too, though it is said that one shaft was in fact made for the convenience of the smugglers. To get back to your car you may prefer to return up the steps, but if you pick your way carefully it is possible to scramble around the rocks below the headland and get to the top by means of the wooden and stone stairs called Tamblyn Way; alternatively, you could wade across the stream and return to the car park across the beach.

PERRANPORTH INFORMATION CENTRE

This is close to the main car park near the beach, beside the entrance to the Seiners' Arms Hotel (close by on your left at the end of this walk). Mrs Lawrence is a mine of general information about the Perranporth area and also holds a good stock of local maps and books - including Landfall Walks Books, of course! The normal opening hours are Monday to Friday 9.30-12.30 and 2.00-4.30, Saturday 9.30-12.30 only. Mrs Lawrence can be contacted by telephone on 01872-573368.

PERRANZABULOE FOLK MUSEUM

If, as I hope, doing walks such as this one has whetted your appetite for local history, I strongly recommend a visit to the excellent Perranzabuloe Folk Museum. It's not far from the main car park at Perranporth, and since there's very little parking space at the museum it's best to walk there. To do so, go back to the bridge, turn left along the main street (St Piran's Road) and then left again at Ponsmere Road. You will soon come to the public library, on your right, and the museum is on the first floor of the same building. Thanks to grant aid, during 2004 it has been enlarged and refurbished. It contains a wealth of fascinating material given or lent by local people, including some fine displays of mining photographs and artefacts. There is a model of St Piran's Oratory, and a full-scale replica of a Cornish cottage kitchen in late Victorian times. Normal opening hours are: Easter to end April: 10am to 1pm and 2 to 4.30pm on Tuesday and Friday, plus Saturday morning. 1st May till late October: daily, excluding Sunday, at the same times. Admission is free.

WALK 8
IN AND AROUND ST AGNES VILLAGE
About 3 miles

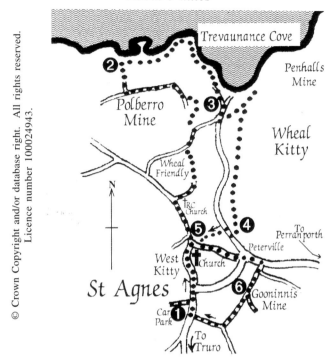

A short walk, but full of interest, with fine views both coastal and inland.

Few Cornish villages - especially villages as attractive as this - are so dominated by the surface relics of mining. The walk visits or passes very close to five imposing engine houses, plus dozens of other associated buildings and workings, some of the latter being extremely ancient. (Basic facts about the mines on this route are given here, but consult *Exploring Cornish Mines* Volumes 1 and 3 if you want the details of their history and technical information about their engines etc., plus photographs old and new.) You will also see what little remains of the harbour built mainly to serve the mines.

There are two quite steep climbs. It should be reasonably dry underfoot all the way. St Agnes has toilets, pubs and shops; there are also toilets, cafés and a pub near the beach at Trevaunance Cove.

The walk starts and ends at the St Agnes car park, Trelawny Road. For instructions on driving there from Truro, see page 90.

ST AGNES AND ITS CHURCH

There has been a church here since at least the 14th century, but little apart from the base of the tower remains of any old building, although some of its stone was used when it was rebuilt on a larger scale in 1848 by J.P.St Aubyn, the highly industrious Victorian architect who has left his mark on almost every old church in the County. (This was two years after the creation of St Agnes parish; till then, this had been a daughter church of Perranzabuloe.) As with so many other Cornish mining communities, the mid-19th century was a period of great expansion in population. The highest census figure for the population of St Agnes was 7,757, in 1841. A market house used to stand where the lych gate is now, but was demolished in 1894 so that the road could be widened. Clive Benney in his 1850-1920 volume tells the story of the "fireball" which struck the spire at St Agnes in 1905; and in 1929 lightning again struck: "the top of the spire, weighing over half a ton, was hurled eastwards about ten feet and fell, after smashing the roof, in one solid mass. Not a stone of it was loosened by the fall and it was later placed outside the south porch of the church." (Quoted from "A Portrait of a Village Church", the interesting booklet which may be available in the church.) Granite blocks from the destroyed harbour were used to build the high altar.

St Agnes was a Roman martyr of the 4th century; whether she had any connection at all with this village or this church is very doubtful, although several local legends exist which refer to her, notably the one telling how she was wooed by the giant Bolster, who could step in one stride from St Agnes Beacon to Carn Brea. The red stain on the side of a crevice above the sea at Chapel Porth was, it is said, caused when she tricked him into trying to fill it with his own blood: only on that condition would she be his bride. The crevice, of course, was holed at the bottom. For the likely origin of the name Bolster, see the note on page 99.

Some say that the original dedication of the church was to St Ann, who had Irish connections, like most of the other saints of North Cornwall, but no written evidence exists of such a dedication; more likely, "Ann" is merely a dialect form of "Agnes". The suggestion that "St Ann" was a corruption of "San Tan" (Celtic, "sacred fire") has been discredited.

Most of the older guide books state that the local people refer to the village as "St Ann's". An old name for it was "Bryanek", with many variant spellings. Thomas Tonkin, back in about 1720, had suggested that this meant "the Village under the Hill", but later changed his mind and decided on "a Place Where Rushes Grow, for such it was within the memory of man, before the adits drained it." John King tentatively explains the old name as "Town of Spar Stone or burying place," and Nicholas Johnson offers "peaked hill, prominent hill" ("Cornish Archaeology", 1980). Oliver Padel, the leading authority on Cornish place-names, is unable to explain the name beyond translating the first syllable as "hill". Just in case you're not sufficiently confused already by this plethora of possible meanings, Ann Preston-Jones has put forward the attractive theory that "St Agnes" may have originated as "Stênes", meaning "place of tin".

1 Return to the main street and turn left. (For information about the West Kitty Thomas' Shaft engine house, close to the car park, and about the Miners' and Mechanics' Institute, see pages 90-91.) **Continue through the centre of St Agnes and turn left on to Trevaunance Road, which is just past the parish church.** On the right a short way along Trevaunance Road is Castle House. According to Maurice Bizley it was once an inn, and there are traditions that it acted as a refuge during the Civil War for either Prince Charles or his brother James, and that a tunnel links it to the Vicarage garden next door. Prospect House, on the left a little further along, is the former count house of West Kitty mine. Just behind it is Reynold's Shaft, where there was a 50-inch pumping engine. The engine house was demolished some twenty years ago to make way for housing.

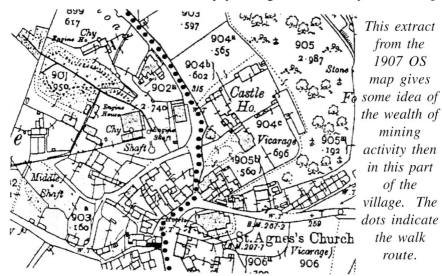

This extract from the 1907 OS map gives some idea of the wealth of mining activity then in this part of the village. The dots indicate the walk route.

WALK 8

Immediately after the Roman Catholic Church, consecrated in 1958, turn right on a track which soon brings you to the splendid engine house and other old buildings of Wheal Friendly, spectacularly situated with Trevaunance Cove as a backdrop, and the buildings of Wheal Kitty and Polberro Mine dominating the skyline to the east and west respectively. (My sketch shows Wheal Kitty as seen from the Wheal Friendly house.)

WHEAL FRIENDLY

Although not a very successful mine, if the surviving records are a fair indication (only 450 tons of copper and about the same amount of tin over a period of some fifty years), quite a lot of its buildings and other relics such as leats have survived in good condition. Wheal Friendly was linked with West Kitty mine. Roger Radcliffe has passed on to me what he was told by the late Bill Harper, who used to live on the site of the old West Kitty Mine. His father worked at Wheal Friendly. It was such a wet mine that on one occasion when the pumping engine had stopped for some reason there was a very rapid inflow of water in the deep part where he was working. He hurried away from his place of work and had to swim the last few feet to the ladderway by the time he arrived at the shaft. The mine's name means "rich" or "profitable": compare all the mines named "Wheal Prosper". Such names were, no doubt, intended to encourage adventurers to provide the necessary investment.

Continue down the narrow path which starts beside the entrance to a walled yard - in fact this was once the mine's water reservoir; water for it was pumped from the mine and ducted in from West Kitty across the fields. The path next passes the remains of one wall of another engine house. This was for a horizontal whim and/or pneumatic stamps engine. **A few steps take you down to another path; turn left on that.** It descends into a little valley which was once the deer park belonging to the Tonkin family of Trevaunance Manor - more about them later. The site of the manor house is a little way up to the left. **At the road, Rocky Lane, turn right, and then almost immediately left, where there is a sign, Public Footpath to Polberro. You pass beside a metal gate to the right of the**

entrances to **Little Orchard Village. After a row of fir trees on your left, the path continues ahead beside a wire fence, quite steeply uphill.** Soon you will see evidence of old mining all around, in the form of capped shafts and the disturbed ground left by surface workings. **When you reach the wider track near the top, turn right.** The fine view to the right along here includes the seaward end of Trevellas Coombe, just beyond the rocky foreshore at the far end of the Trevaunance Cove beach. **Continue until you reach an old chimney stack.** This was part of Polberro Mine; look left for a good view of the Turnavore Shaft engine-house, with its corrugated-asbestos roof.

(Beside it are large concrete dressing floors with several convex buddles, shown in my drawing. Unfortunately, the track leading past these to the engine house is private. A similar area of dressing floors is to be seen at Wheal Kitty, later on this walk; in fact, the dressing floors at Polberro were transferred from Wheal Kitty in about 1937.)

POLBERRO MINE

Peter Stanier states that Polberro was "once the richest mine in Cornwall". This mining area is certainly one of the most ancient and intensively worked in Cornwall, and doubtless gave rise to the old Cornish saying, "Stean San Agnes an guella stean en Kernow", "St Agnes tin is the finest tin in Cornwall." According to R. H. Bird, the mine was renamed "Polberro Royal Consols" after a visit by Queen Victoria in 1846; but when it was advertised for sale in the "West Briton" in 1843 it was already called "Royal Polberou Consols". One suggestion is that it had produced silver for the Royal Mint. Polberro's main period of activity was from 1837 to 1895, and the surviving engine house was built in 1887 for a 60-inch engine which had previously been at South Penstruthal Mine (Lanner) and before that at North Pool. From Polberro the engine made one more move, a short one this time to Wheal Friendly. The Turnavore Shaft was re-opened from 1937 to 1941 and deepened to over a thousand feet. The plant at that time was all electrical, and the old engine house was roofed to provide a changing-house for the miners. (The name, by the way, like Polperro, seems to mean "Peter's pool".)

WALK 8

Just before the stack, turn right on to a track that leads down to the cliff edge. The stack belonged to an arsenic burning house, and was originally taller, with a brick top section. The lack of any remains of a "lambreth" flue suggests that no attempt was made to collect the arsenic.

2 Turn right on the coast path. The cliff scenery is splendid here - but notice too, on your right, all the waste heaps and capped shafts, the remains of very ancient mining. One particularly deep hollow on the inland side of the path looks like the work of miners following a mineralised lode. Before long, as you approach a headland, you will see a concrete leat leading to the cliff edge. This originally ran from the dressing floors at Turnavore, Polberro. If you walk (carefully!) to the far end of it and look at the cliff face to your left, you will see the mouth of an adit from Polberro about half way up the cliff. A little lower down the path, just before the main flight of steps, there is another adit portal on your right. Near the foot of the steps are the remains of storage "hutches" - rather similar to the eight hutches at Devoran Quay: see *Exploring Cornwall's Tramway Trails*, Volume 2, page 193 - which are now the clearest evidence that St Agnes once had a harbour. Just before the path passes through a gap on the left side of a metal gate, look inland to see an upper section of the concrete leat or aqueduct from Turnavore, and below it a fine example of "old men's workings". The cavernous hollow is wholly man-made, part of the excavations of an old mine called Wheal Luna. (To get closer to it you have to fight your way through an ever-thickening forest of Japanese Knotweed; a wooden fence discourages further progress into a space which is probably subject to dangerous rock-falls.)

As you walk on, you soon pass what used to be the Trevaunance Point Hotel, now converted into holiday apartments. Down on the beach is a scattering of large granite blocks, all that remains of the last harbour.

ST AGNES HARBOUR

As the centre of a busy mining district at a time when inland transport varied from difficult to impossible, St Agnes urgently needed a harbour, and from 1632 onwards at least five attempts were made to build one, but sea storms always won in the end. The one which lasted easily the longest was built in 1793 at a cost, according to Murray's Handbook for Devon and Cornwall (1859), of £10,000; it survived intact till 1915, but during that summer one stone in the North Quay was washed away; the damage was not repaired, and an autumn gale breached the wall. By 1924, the

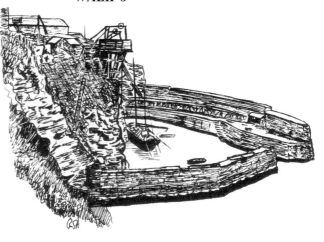

once impressive harbour was reduced to a heap of stones. Several photos exist, however (one of which was the basis for this drawing), showing the two quays protecting a space big enough for about six coasting ships.

Apart from a narrow flight of steps and a ladderway, there was no access to the quays from inland. Ore from the storage hutches was loaded on to the vessels by two long chutes, and incoming cargoes had to be lifted in baskets or "kibbles" attached to ropes which passed over pulleys on a wooden platform built out over the cliff edge. These were operated by two horsewhims about thirty feet from the edge.

The principal uses of the harbour were for the shipping out of copper ore for smelting in South Wales and the import of coal for the mine engines, but it also allowed a pilchard fishery to be established.

The bulk of the St Agnes Museum Trust's Journal No.6 (1990) is devoted to studies of the harbour and its history by Roger Radcliffe and Ann Preston-Jones. The scale model of St Agnes harbour at the local museum is excellent, and gives a clearer impression than words or even maps and photographs can of how it was designed and operated. (Some information about the museum is given at the end of the directions for this walk.)

Late in the 1990s a body named the St Agnes Harbour Trust was set up with the aim of creating a new working harbour at the cove. The estimated cost was £3 million. Early in 1999 the local press reported, under the banner "Harbour dream may be realised", that the project was "entirely feasible" in engineering terms, but in September 2002 the headline was "No go for village harbour plan". By then the cost estimate was £5 million, and attempts to secure both public and private funding had met with insufficient success.

Continue along the wide track, which will soon bring you down to the road close to Trevaunance beach. The garden of the bungalow on the far side of the small car park on your left as you approach the road marks the site where, late in the 1950s, Ken Jones created a small pool to accommodate seals rescued along the coast nearby. This was how the Cornish Seal Sanctuary originated. As more and more seals arrived, a much bigger pool was needed; by 1969 even this was inadequate, and the search began for a new site. The Sanctuary at Gweek (see *Around the Helford*, page 46) was first opened to the public in 1975.

It is worth going down to the beach to see the mouth of the main Polberro adit gushing water on the left. (An interesting old photograph of this adit is included in *Bygone Cornwall* - details on page 54 - showing the large group of mine buildings at Wheal Friendly in the background and a tin recovery plant building overshadowing the beach.) The cliff on the right is dominated by the spoil heaps of Penhalls Mine and Wheal Kitty, and less than half-way up the cliff-face below them is another adit-mouth.

3 Walk up the road, and turn left on to the coast path just before you reach the Driftwood Spars Hotel. (During the 19th century this building was used as a store for the mines and other industries in the valley.) The climb is quite stiff, and you may well be glad of the seat at the top; from here you have a fine view of the site of the harbour, as well as Wheal Friendly and Polberro. **To inspect the surface remains of Wheal Kitty, take the path on the right - not the one signposted to St Agnes, but the rougher track heading towards the engine house.** The square chimney stack over to the left was part of an arsenic plant belonging to Penhalls Mine. Ahead is a large waste heap. To the left and on the far side of that are extensive concrete dressing floors dating from early in the 20th century (photograph overleaf), with several good examples of convex buddles.

The much more ruinous remains of the 19th-century floors are over to the right, on the slope overlooking Trevaunance Coombe. The engine house on Sara's Shaft used to be surrounded by buildings dating from the late 1920s, when Wheal Kitty was last worked, but since buying the site in 1997 Carrick District Council has developed the Wheal Kitty Industrial Estate. Some of the mine buildings have been demolished, others converted into workshops or, more recently, offices. In 2004 it was announced that the site was "to have a £900,000 facelift", and by

Wheal Kitty's 20th-century dressing floors photographed in 1993, with the buildings around Sara's Shaft behind

early 2005 the engine house had been fully renovated externally, with new windows, doors, roof and bob plat (the wooden maintenance platform near the top of the bob wall), and its interior converted into office space.

WHEAL KITTY

This was one of the most important of St Agnes' mines, producing, according to the surviving records, 13,121 tons of tin and 2,024 tons of copper between 1834 and 1930. Like nearly all these enterprises, it was an amalgamation of many smaller mines, some very ancient. The Sara's Shaft house contained a 65-inch pumping engine. In 1905 the stamps engine house, which stood among the older dressing floors a little to the south-west of Sara's Shaft, was burnt down, probably as a result of arson by a sacked official. The engine itself and part of the bob wall survived, and the old photo reproduced in my drawing gives some idea of how a beam engine was used to provide rotative power.

WALK 8

Return to the coast path and take the inland path signposted to St Agnes, which provides you with fine views over Trevaunance Coombe. Photograph 89 in Trounson's book (details, page 160) makes an interesting comparison with the scene today. One of the most notable sons of St Agnes parish was the historian Thomas Tonkin (1678-1742); he was born at Trevaunance Manor, on the other side of the valley, and it was his family who had pioneered early attempts to build a harbour at Trevaunance Porth. The clatter of machinery must have dominated life in the Coombe in his day, for he writes, "The water arising on Trevaunance, in conjunction with Breanick (St Agnes) water-course, drives twelve stamping mills, and a griest mill ..." and he adds, "There was formerly in Trevaunance Coom a blowing house with anothor griest mill ..." A century or more after his death there were a hammer mill and an iron foundry in the valley. **The path eventually descends to the road.**

4 Turn right. Please take extreme care on this road, which is narrow and can be quite busy, especially in the summer. After a few yards, you will probably be able to take the path on the left, signed to Glen Cottage. This has been in general use by walkers for many years, but is not strictly a right of way, so you may instead have to walk further down the road (passing, on your left, the site of the former iron foundry) **till you come to a public seat on the left, where another path begins, cutting back sharply. Both these routes soon cross a stream, pass beside Glen Cottage, and take you up beside the much-photographed row of cottages called Stippy Stappy.** Older names were Bosun's Row or simply Cottage Row.

5 At the road, you could turn right to return directly to the car park, but if you are not already tired of looking at old mines, turn left and walk down to Peterville - an area which in the days before motorised traffic provided a useful open space for village events. It was once graced with the name "Dirtypool". Dirtypool Forge, which then stood opposite what is now the Peterville Inn, and the Dirty Pool Malting Co., which formerly supplied malt for brewing to the local pubs, perhaps created much of the dirt. At various times there were also a cobbler, a wheelwright and a carpenter. Where Images of Cornwall and the Saffron Gallery now stand was once a lime pit. One of the photographs in Clive Benney's earlier volume shows Peterville in about 1905, with a coalyard on one side and the Reynold's Shaft engine house of West Kitty, complete with headgear, towering above. In 2003, Dawn Woon published an interesting little book, *Memories of Peterville*, which includes more old photos. She mentions the suggestion that the modern name derives from a prominent man, Hugh Peter, who lived hereabouts in the 18th century; I'm tempted to wonder whether the name "Polberro" also has some link with his family. (See the end of the note about Polberro mine.) **Just beyond the pub** ("The Victoria" in Dirtypool days), **take the second turning on the right, which heads towards Goonown and Goonbell.**

6 **After passing the Rosevean Hotel, fork left up a small side road leading to the Mount Pleasant nursing home.** The farm track on the left at the top leads to the remains of Gooninnis Mine, which suffered damage during the winter of 1992-3, when lightning struck the engine-house stack. Repairs were carried out late in 1994. The buildings belong to the Duchy of Cornwall, but are on private land owned by Mr Roy Blewett, who tells me he has no objection to visitors inspecting them, so long as they do not tamper with farm or stable equipment, and securely fasten the gate on leaving.

GOONINNIS MINE

The remains of this mine, with its two castellated stacks, are all the more impressive in view of the fact that Gooninnis (often spelt Gooninis) was only a trial working in search of tin. It started in 1873 but was most active between 1899 and 1907. The 50-inch pumping engine, after several years at Trevaunance Mine (Walk 9), was operating here by 1901 and removed in 1910. No record exists of any actual output; its lodes were linked to those of Wheal Kitty, and its returns were included in those of the larger mine. In an area as intensively mined as this, workings inevitably overlapped: apparently West Kitty, Wheal Kitty and Blue Hills - see Walk 7 - all interconnected underground. If you can get hold of the St Agnes - Perranporth volume of A. K. Hamilton Jenkin's "Mines and Miners of Cornwall", now out of print, look at the map on page 29, dating from 1838, which shows the complex pattern of setts in this area. The harbour and hutches at Trevaunance Cove are also shown. Clive Benney's 1850- 1920 volume includes interesting photographs showing Gooninnis; one of them illustrates well how massive the steam-engine bobs (beams) were. It shows the bob being removed to Castle an Dinas, near St Columb Major, in 1911; the engine, with a new bob, still survives at Goonvean Clay Pit. (The name, Gooninnis, is also that of a nearby farm; it probably means "isolated, remote spot on the down": "innis" seems to derive from enys or ynys, literally an island. Goon, meaning "down" or "rough

WALK 8

grazing land" is a common element in place-names around St Agnes: Goonbell, "distant downs", Goonvrea, "hilly pasture", and Goonlaze, "green down", are some. "Goonvean" means "small downland.")

Return to the road at the bottom, turn left, and then take the first right turning, passing the Rosemundy House Hotel. According to Dawn Woon this "was at one time a brewery" and later the place "where unmarried mothers had their babies". "Rosemundy" is a name that reflects the importance of mining in the story of St Agnes: *ros mon-dy*, "moorland mineral house", by which I suppose is meant an ore-bin. **This road brings you to the main street opposite the Railway Inn; here turn right, and for the car park turn left.**

THE RAILWAY INN

This dates back to the 17th century, and was originally called The Smith's Arms, because there was a smithy behind it. A shaft of an old mine called Polbreen is also behind the inn, and there is a legend that the workings nearby are haunted by the ghost of Dorcas, a girl who committed suicide by jumping into the shaft after her fiancé died in a mining accident. The story also tells how the ghost once saved a young miner underground by calling him away from a spot where the roof was just about to cave in. "At certain times," writes Frank Pearce in the old guide book from which I have taken all the above information about the inn, "the sound of the sea can still be heard through the tunnels under 'The Railway'."

In 1904, when the railway line reached St Agnes, the name was altered to The Smith's Arms and Railway Hotel. The inn was not, in fact, very close to the railway, which ran nearly a mile south of the village, and crossed the main road towards Truro on a bridge whose remains are still a prominent landmark, as seen in my sketch.

The station was near the bridge, at Great Western Railway Yard, and its main building is still easily recognisable, converted for use as industrial units; there was also a halt at Goonbell. (The diesel shunter engine on display beside St Agnes station probably dates from the 1960s. It had previously been bought by someone at Goonhavern who had plans to develop part of the old railway line there as a tourist attraction.) The line from near Chacewater to Perranporth was opened in 1903, and two years later it reached Newquay. Although it was well-used by holidaymakers, it was "axed" by Dr Beeching in 1963. Its track would have made a fine footpath, but it was sold off piecemeal, and much of it is now covered with rubbish or gorse and brambles.

ST AGNES MUSEUM

Before you leave St Agnes, if you are at all interested in industrial archaeology and local history - and I don't think you would be reading this book otherwise - you should make a point of visiting the museum. Originally the collection was housed at Peterville, but since 1991 it has occupied a former chapel at the village cemetery on Penwinnick Road. It is on the left as you enter St Agnes from the south, just before the turning to Chapel Porth, and only 250 yards from the main car park. (Please note that there is no parking at the museum itself.) Opening hours are from 10.30am to 5pm every day including Sundays from 1st April to the end of September. Admission is free. Among the displays is a huge leatherback turtle which was washed up on Porthtowan beach. One of the latest acquisitions is the figurehead of a schooner, the "Lady Agnes", built locally in the 1870s; the volunteers who run the museum raised £18,000 to buy the figurehead. The museum focuses especially on local minerals and mining, and has an interesting video about the tin streaming still being practised at Blue Hills: see Walk 7. As mentioned earlier, there is a most impressive model of the old harbour. The St Agnes Museum Trust has published fifteen annual journals which contain many fascinating articles, often of special interest to the industrial archaeologist.

WALK 9
ST AGNES, NEWDOWNS HEAD, CHAPEL PORTH
& ST AGNES BEACON
A selection of walks ranging from about 6 to under 2 miles

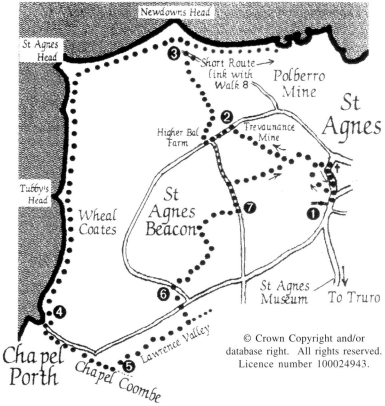

There are few Cornish headlands more spectacular than St Agnes Head, few mine buildings more wonderfully situated than Wheal Coates. Chapel Coombe is well worth a second visit, and the little valley that follows it on the walk is one of those charmed spots that nestle among hillsides bare but for the ever-glowing gorse. Finally, as a reminder of the title of this book in its original form, there is "a view from St Agnes Beacon"! For detailed information about the mines in this area, see *Exploring Cornish Mines*, Volumes 3 and 4.

You will probably need waterproof footwear for that valley; elsewhere you are mostly on well-made tracks and quiet roads. In St Agnes there are shops and pubs, and toilets and refreshments are available - often even in the dead of winter - at Chapel Porth.

Four possible routes are suggested:

For the full six-mile walk park either in St Agnes or at Chapel Porth. The car park at Chapel Porth is free to National Trust members.

For a walk of just under five miles, omitting St Agnes, start at Chapel Porth.

For the shortest walks (about three miles or under two miles), both omitting Chapel Porth, start at St Agnes. Note that the three-mile walk partly repeats the route of Walk 8.

To drive to St Agnes from Truro, take the A390 westwards to the Chiverton Cross roundabout and follow the St Agnes sign from there. The car park (still free in 2004) is on Trelawney Road, to the left just after you enter the main street.

To drive to Chapel Porth, turn left at the mini-roundabout at the start of the main street. Chapel Porth is signed from there. If you are basing the walk on Chapel Porth, pick up the directions at point 4.

1 From the St Agnes car park, return to the main street and turn left. Notice the Miners' and Mechanics' Institute on the left.

ST AGNES MINERS' & MECHANICS' INSTITUTE

Above the date, 1893, are the initials JPE. John Passmore Edwards is a name you will see on many public buildings, especially libraries, in Cornwall; he also established hospitals, art galleries, technical schools and colleges, including some in London, and endowed an English scholarship at Oxford. He was born nearby at Blackwater in 1823, the son of a carpenter, and began by selling strawberries when his father turned to market gardening. Later he became involved in journalism in London, and after several loss-making ventures he made a success of "Building News", and later bought the "Echo", the first halfpenny newspaper. He was a well-known champion of causes such as Early Closing and Anti-Gambling, and as a pacifist he denounced the Crimean and Boer Wars. He was Liberal MP for Salisbury from 1880 to 1885, and died in 1911. He twice refused a knighthood. He once offered to build a lighthouse on St Agnes Beacon, but the authorities (The Trinity Brethren) did not feel that one was required there; they also said that if it was erected the light would be so high that it would be sometimes lost in the mists. When Edwards laid the foundation stone at the St Agnes Institute, a "time capsule" containing coins, newspapers and a programme of the day's events was placed beneath it; Clive Benney in his earlier volume tells how it was stolen a few days later and afterwards replaced with a new one. (In 1993 the St Agnes Museum Trust published a booklet about John Passmore Edwards and the Institute in celebration of its centenary.)

Soon after this, turn left opposite Pengarth Road to get a good view of the Thomas' Shaft pumping-engine house and nearby stack - parts of West Kitty mine.

WEST KITTY

This mine in the centre of St Agnes began in 1863 and worked until 1916. It produced a little copper, but mainly tin ore, which was taken to the stamps at Jericho (Walk 7) for crushing. West Kitty was formed from several older mines, in one of which the mineral called stannite, tin pyrites or bell-metal ore was discovered in about 1785; this is much rarer than the usual tin-bearing ore, cassiterite. The discoverer was a German, Rudolf Erich Raspe, best known as the author of the fantastic stories of the travels of Baron Munchausen, which he wrote when he was storekeeper at Dolcoath Mine, Camborne. The original steam engine which pumped water from the Thomas section of West Kitty was later employed at Carpalla china clay works and is still preserved - though in bits and unrestored - in a store at the Science Museum, South Kensington. The Thomas Shaft engine house was repaired and made safe by Carrick District Council in 1990.

Turn right at the T-junction, go along the path and road (Angwin Avenue) into the council estate, turn right at the next T-junction (Trelawney Road), bear right into Beaconsfield Place, and then left at the old cottage on the left, Bramble Cottage. When you come to a stile ahead, don't cross it but turn right and walk between hedges. Now you come to another stile; cross that, go through the kissing-gate, and then head just left of the stack to a further stile at the field corner. After a rather muddy stretch you cross another stile; keep heading slightly left of the stack to cross yet another stile, and then turn right, passing the chimney. This and the ivy-covered ruined buildings nearby are parts of Trevaunance Mine. **Continue to the road.**

TREVAUNANCE MINE

Known at various times as Wheal Trevaunance and Trevaunance Consols or Trevaunance United (when it joined forces with Goonlaze Mine), this was "*a very ancient and profitable mine, said to have given £100,000 in dividends*" (Collins). *Both tin and copper were produced, and it worked continuously for 150 years. An interesting article by Roger Radcliffe in the first Journal of the St Agnes Museum Trust focuses on the early history of Wheal Trevaunance. Just how old the mine is is uncertain, but the neighbouring Pell Mine was active as early as 1511, and there are records of the driving of adits by Wheal Trevaunance in the 1720s and 1775. Mr Radcliffe illustrates his claim that in the latter part of the 19th century Trevaunance was "perhaps the most primitive mine in the county" by the fact that steam power did not reach it till the 1880s; until then, any workings below adit were, it seems, drained "by means of barrels hauled by windlass, or later by horse whim" and perhaps also by hand pumps. The big beam engines were commonly moved from site to site according to demand, and the Gooninnis engine (see page 86) worked here between 1884 and 1900. The low building is the remains of the whim engine house; the engine was completely enclosed, like the recently restored one at Levant (see "Around Land's End", Walk 7), and came from Wheal Coates nearby. H.G.Ordish's 1967 volume has a photograph of the engine houses as they were in 1935. The stack of the 50-inch pumping engine house remains, but the rest of the building was pronounced unsafe and demolished in 1984. The St Agnes Museum Trust secured the preservation of what you now see.*

2 **To see what remains of the whim-engine house, turn right; its base is still just visible amid the undergrowth behind the seat in the layby.** Notice, on the opposite side of the road, the huge area of waste heaps and shafts, relics of the great Polberro Mine (page 80). **But to continue the walk, turn left on reaching the road and continue as far as the left turning to The Beacon and Mingoose.**

Here, if you started in St Agnes, you could make a very short walk of it by taking this left turning and then, after a little under a quarter of a mile, crossing the stile on the left where there is a sign, Public Footpath to the Village. From there, follow the directions in point 7, starting at line 7: "For a little over 100 yards ...".

To continue to Chapel Porth, or to complete the three-mile walk based on St Agnes, take the track on the right, beside Higher Bal Farm. At the small chapel, now a house, bear right. Ignore the side tracks on the left; keep to the main one, which bends left and passes a bungalow;

ignore the left turning, to New Downs Farm, and follow the track round to the right till you reach a road. Here turn left, passing the depot of Doble Quality Foods (or, more accurately, doble quality foods). When you reach the sign of Bawden Manor Farm, take the grassy path on the right, signed "To the Coast Path". The seat here makes a good opportunity for a picnic stop: the view in clear conditions extends along the coast past Cligga Head, Perran Sands, Ligger and Penhale Points to the lighthouse at Trevose. Inland can be seen the tall windmills at Carland Cross and other sites; and you may well have the gliders from Trevellas airfield to entertain you. **The path soon brings you down to the coast.**

3 For the other short walk turn right on the coast path. The first section of it is dominated by the old workings of Polberro Mine. After about half a mile, when you see a mine stack quite close, up on your right, pick up the directions given for Walk 8 at point 2 (page 81).

For the full walk to Chapel Porth and the Beacon, turn left on the coast path, passing the National Trust sign, Newdowns Head. From here if you look back you will see two capped mineshafts, and indeed almost everywhere along this part of the coast there is evidence of mining, particularly as you approach St Agnes Head. **Follow the acorn signs.** The coast path keeps to the seaward side of the St Agnes Head coastguard lookout. Just as you are about to reach the Head itself there is a small quarry on the left where drilled holes can be seen in the rock face. At the headland are concrete remains, presumably relics of World War 2 coastal defences. During the war the area immediately inland from here was an army camp; in 1949 it was taken over by the local council and the buildings were let to families on the waiting list for council houses. The story of the Cameron Estate is told by Dawn Woon in a small book published in 2002. Little if anything remains now, apart from a few flowers and shrubs marking where the tenants' gardens were.

Further on beyond the Head, where a wall starts on the left, there is a big Clwyd cap over a deep shaft by the cliff edge, with a cobbled area beside it whose purpose I can only guess at. This was probably part of Wheal Bungay, a mine which Collins lists but gives no information on. The famous and highly photogenic clifftop buildings of Wheal Coates now come into view. As you approach them, it is worth following the rough little paths to the left to visit the small stack over there, because this gives you a clear view of the vast amount of openwork mining that took place here before the shafts were sunk.

WHEAL COATES

Wheal Coates was already described as "old" in 1720, but most of the earliest workings must have been by means of gunnises in Towanwroath Vugga (cave) and the cliff face, together with shallow pits and trenches following the lodes inland. By 1828 the mine had acquired a steam engine. During the 1840s a 60" engine was put on sale. The mine had 133 employees in 1847, but was working only above adit level. For most of the 19th century only "a little tin was got from time to time by tributers" (Collins). During the 1870s and 1880s Wheal Coates was worked on a larger scale, and it was then that most of the surviving structures were built, but it was not a particularly successful mine, producing only just over a thousand tons of ore, mainly tin, between 1815 and 1889, with another short period of working just before the First World War. The lower house, on Towanroath Shaft, contained the 30-inch pumping engine. This building was stabilised by the National Trust in 1973, and the stamps engine house above in 1986-8. The site as a whole is relatively complex and difficult to understand, but the "interpretive" board provided by the Trust is helpful, and if you are keen to learn more, I recommend "Exploring Cornish Mines" Volume 4, and the detailed study by the Cornwall Archaeological Unit: see the Further Reading section. At low tide it is worth going down to the beach (from Chapel Porth) to see the lode in the cliff-face and, if the tide is right and you are equipped with a torch, to explore the cave, at the back of which water still issues from the mouth of the adit. The lode has been extensively stoped in the roof of the cave.

The signed coastal footpath now descends to the lower engine house. If you prefer to continue to the upper group of buildings - well worth a close look if you are interested in mining history - you can still get to the Towanroath Shaft site from there, but the path down is quite steep and rough. The upper buildings include the stabilised, three-storeyed stamps engine house with the smaller building behind it that housed the whim, and behind that the more modern horizontal whim. Just south of the buildings is a well-preserved mine pond, and on the seaward side are the remains of dressing floors, including a ruined burning house or calciner. The sturdy chimney stack at the top - originally much taller - served that as well as the boiler house for the stamps and whim engines.

Best-known of all is the 30-inch pumping engine house below at Towanroath Shaft. Even more popular with photographers than the group

Wheal Coates: the Towanroath Shaft engine house, photographed by Simon Vere Jones

above, it was chosen as the image for a 1st class stamp, part of the Royal Mail's "British Journey" set issued in 2005. **(The rough path down to it is on the north side of the dressing floors. Alternatively, you could retrace your steps to the point where the coast path makes its descent. If you don't want to go down, clear tracks at the top run roughly parallel with the coast and eventually bring you to the road leading down to the Chapel Porth car park.)** Beside the engine house stands its boiler house, which was modified in 1910 to house a steam pump. ("Towanroath", sometimes spelt "Towanwroath", is the name of the cave below. It means "the hole, or perhaps hollow place, of the hag or witch".)

Now walk on to Chapel Porth, following the coast path acorn signs. When you come to a steep little valley, the path heads inland, then makes a hairpin bend back towards the cliffs. This route brings you to the road just above the car park. Go down to that now.

Towanwroath Vugga, with the 30-inch pumping-engine house on Towanroath Shaft above

If you have not already explored Chapel Porth beach and its caves, it's well worth doing so at low tide; some details are in the note on Wheal Coates (page 94), and on page 112. See also *Exploring Cornish Mines* Volume 4.

WALK 9
CHAPEL PORTH AND CHAPEL COOMBE

The site of "St Agnes Well and Chapel" has been identified on the north side of the cove, and according to a booklet published in 1979 by the Cornwall County Council, "Chapel Porth Nature Trail", a small chapel was dismantled in 1780. The valley was intensively mined from early times, and mine buildings occupied the area which is now the National Trust car park: see the photograph dated 1908 on page 19 of Clive Benney's 1850-1920 book. These, and the remains of buildings, leats and capped shafts further up the Coombe, were workings of mines called Charlotte United, East Charlotte and Wheal Freedom. To quote from the Nature Trail booklet, now regrettably out of print, "Most of the noise in the valley" (that is, while the mines were working) "was caused by the tin crushing machines or 'stamps' which pounded the ore produced by local mines into fine sand. The crushing 'heads' of the stamps were raised by water power. Artificial cuttings or 'leats' channelled the water on to large water wheels. Stream water was supplemented by thousands of gallons pumped up from the lower levels of the mines by the great Cornish Beam engines housed in the weather and time resistant buildings still seen at the head of the valley."

4 The walk up Chapel Coombe starts at the footbridge just to the right of the café. Notice the various shafts and ruinous buildings in the valley. (The sketch, looking up the coombe, shows old masonry on the far side of the stream.) The engine house ahead contained a 30-inch pumping engine and belonged to a mine named on the late 19th-century maps as Charlotte United, though it had started in about 1806 as North Towan, and during its most productive period (c.1830-56) was called New Charlotte. It output was mostly copper. As you cross the wooden footbridge below it, look down on the right to see the mouth of the mine's adit, now flooded. It is worth scrambling up the path just beyond (beside the big waste heap) for a closer look at the engine house, impressively sited against the backdrop of the valley down to the sea; but there are several deep pits around it, so great care is needed. **Continue along the valley path.**

5 After about 250 yards turn left, via a wooden kissing-gate, crossing two streams. Bear right on the main track, and where this bends left at a metal farm gate keep right (almost, in fact, straight ahead), joining a narrower path. It follows a stream, and passes below the dumps of another mine, called East Charlotte. This, together with the neighbouring Wheal Freedom, seems to have worked intermittently over a long period: there are records of sales of small amounts of copper in the 1820s and 1860s and a little tin early this century. Now, when you reach a charming pair of old houses set in superb gardens, suddenly the valley becomes idyllically rural and sheltered, filled with water-sounds and wild flowers: when my wife and I walked there quite early in March, there were already dozens of bluebells in full bloom. You may well be glad of waterproof footwear here: in March, the path itself was one of the streams! Many locals know this little valley as Wheal Lawrence, an interesting corruption of an old name: a spring here was called Venton Aurance, "Silver Spring", so the valley became Arrance Coombe and an old mine here was named Wheal Arrans - thus Lawrence was born. (Thanks to Bill Morrison for that information, which I culled from the 1986 *Journal of the St Agnes Museum Trust.*) **After a gate, the path enters a field and runs beside a barbed-wire fence. Cross the stile on the left by a wooden gate. Go up this track, ignoring a left turning beside a gate marked Willow Cottage. Continue straight ahead at the road, going past a garage and along a narrow path by a wire fence till you reach another road.**

6 Turn left and immediately right up a track signed "Footpath to Beacon". Soon you fork left on to a narrower path which goes to the top of the hill. (This path starts about 20 yards before the main track enters the grounds of a private house.) As you go, look inland to see, on the skyline, Carn Brea crowned with the Basset monument; Carn Marth, the furthest left of the four hills; the woods near Scorrier to the left of that, and further left still the prominent engine house of North Treskerby. On the far right are Trencrom and the other hills south and west of St Ives. When you reach the trig. point at the top (complete with a useful topograph, placed here in 1999) you will, in clear conditions, have a good view of the St Austell china-clay mining area in the east, and the coast north as far as Trevose Head, near Padstow; Perranporth is hidden by Cligga Head. Godrevy lighthouse is a prominent feature in the opposite direction. Close at hand are the St Agnes mines, including Polberro on the cliff-edge and Wheal Kitty just beyond the village.

ST AGNES BEACON

St Agnes Beacon - "a stupendous and amazing high mountain" in the eyes of William Hals (1655-1737) - is like a great island of killas (sedimentary rock) standing above the granite. At or near its top, 630 feet above sea level, are ancient burial mounds. The fact that an earthwork over 3km in length was constructed on the southern side of the hill - apparently linking Chapel Coombe and Trevaunance Coombe - suggests that the area it enclosed had some kind of special importance at one time. The earthwork, part of which has survived to a height of about 11ft from the bottom of the ditch to the top of the rampart, is now known as the Bolster Bank; "Bolster" seems to derive from Cornish words meaning "a hump shaped like a boat". Other names it has been given include Kledh, meaning "dyke", and Gorres, meaning "weir, dam". If you are interested to know more about it, see the article by Nicholas Johnson in "Cornish Archaeology" No. 19 (1980). The purpose of the earthwork and the date of its construction remain matters for speculation. All around the hill, near the top, is a layer of grey clay, used by the early miners to attach tallow candles to their helmets (and I suppose this is the same clay which Thomas Tonkin says was "much used by pipe makers"), and beneath this clay is a stratum of sand and pebbles, showing that millions of years ago the sea must have been at this level, or that earth-movements have lifted the rocks - or that this is the high-tide mark of Noah's Flood, as the old miners apparently held. (Perhaps they got the idea from Tonkin, who wrote that it is "clear evidence of the Deluge".) The clay and sand have both been quarried in recent years, mainly for use in iron foundries. Remains of openwork tin mining, and also stone quarries which supplied the building material for the engine houses, can also be found on the

Beacon. The hill has been quarried in a small way for centuries, and the family doing the quarrying now have been involved for over 150 years. From the top of St Agnes Beacon can be seen, it is claimed, 30 church towers, as well as ships at anchor in Falmouth Bay, and the top of St Michael's Mount: a perfect site for the beacon fires lit in times of emergency or rejoicing. Even Carn Brea, Carn Marth, Trencrom and Carn Galver (all of which have figured in the titles of earlier Landfall Walks Books) cannot beat it as a place to stand and reflect on Cornwall's industrial past, and what its future may hold.

From the top, take the path leading down towards St Agnes; it curves left and right before reaching a road.

7 Turn left along the road.

If you started at Chapel Porth and don't want to include St Agnes in the walk, continue along the road till you come to a T-junction. There, take the track almost opposite, beside Higher Bal Farm, and pick up the directions at the last two lines of page 92.

For St Agnes: just past the group of houses, turn right over a stile by a sign, Public Footpath to the Village. For a little over 100 yards, keep by the wall on your left; then cross the stile on your right. The path crosses the centre of the field to another stile, then runs between hedges. After that, keep by the hedge on the left, cross two more stiles beside farm gates, and continue ahead on the wide track. At the road, go straight on down the path, to emerge near the church on the main street. Turn right to return to the car park.

WALK 10
PORTHTOWAN, MINGOOSE & CHAPEL PORTH
About 6½ miles - shorter if you omit Tywarnhayle Mine

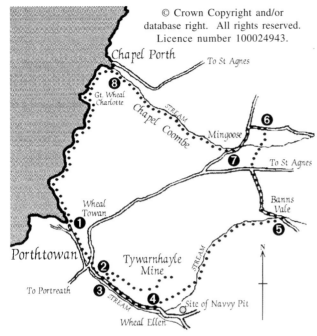

Here is another walk which takes in quite a tough section of the coastal path with fine scenery and views. An "optional extra" on this walk is to explore the surface remains of Tywarnhayle, a large and important copper mine with one of Cornwall's most dramatically situated inland engine houses. Although this book gives a "guided tour" of Tywarnhayle, those wanting more information and a plan of the site should refer to *Exploring Cornish Mines* Volume 1. Similarly, the interesting evidence of mining in and around Chapel Porth is fully described and explained in Volume 4.

Like several other walks in this book, this one offers a strong contrast between the coastal and inland sections: as you wander along the pretty valley called "shady walk", or through the picturesque hamlet of Mingoose, it is almost incredible that those fearsome cliffs are hardly a mile away.

There is some road walking, and the road between points 1 and 4 can be quite busy. The path has sticky patches. There are toilets, shops, a pub and several other eateries at Porthtowan; at Echo Corner, near point 2, is the Avalon restaurant; and not far from the suggested route is the Victory Inn, which offers a varied and imaginative menu. The National Trust Beach Café at Chapel Porth (to quote my Gastronomy Correspondent, Gill Jacobs) "does wonderful food - garlic bread, croque monsieur and home-made ices." Their "Hedgehogs", liberally plastered with Cornish cream, are particularly memorable, but not conducive to vigorous walking!

WALK 10

To drive to Porthtowan from St Agnes, take the B33277 road towards Truro, turning sharp right after about a mile and a half. From the coast road above Porthtowan take the turning (again sharp right) down to the village and beach. Coming frorn Truro, take the A390 westwards; at the roundabout where this meets the A30 (Three Burrows or Chiverton roundabout) follow the sign to St Agnes, and after about two miles turn left. From there continue as described above. There are car parks on the right near The Unicorn (former Commodore Inn) and by the beach.

PORTHTOWAN

A predecessor of mine, Victor Thursby, published in 1932 a little book called "Fourteen Hikes along the Cornish Coast", which is full of surprising observations. "Three miles from the start," he writes, "one comes to the quaint little village of Porth Towan, which strongly resembles Portreath." An interesting photograph on page 30 in Clive Benney's earliest volume shows a corn mill and attractive cottages close to where the Post Office now is, but that picture dates from 1904 - well before Mr Thursby's time. Had he actually been there? Or have seventy-odd years wrought even more dramatic changes to the Cornish landscape than I realised? "Quaint" is about the last adjective I'd have chosen for Porthtowan, and it would be quite low on the list for Portreath. There are, of course, a few substantial houses among the temporary-looking structures which have clustered around Porthtowan's fine beach, a favourite among surfers; one of the buildings, in fact, was a mine's engine house, as explained at the end of the directions. By the late 1990s Porthtowan had become very run-down, with buildings such as the village hall and the closed-down Porpoise Inn suffering from vandalism, and the chalets of a former holiday camp at Porthvale turned into a "Ghetto" seething with social problems and looking more and more like a scrap-metal dump. Since then, great improvements have come about: new housing on and near the Porpoise site, a new village hall, new shops, and much more. At the time of writing, the Porthvale chalets have been cleared and planning approval for more housing is awaited. Some local residents would prefer the site to be used for an overflow car park.

Although the name "Porthtowan" is recorded as far back as 1628, at that time there seem to have been only tin-stamps here: the village itself began to appear only 150 or 200 years later with the great growth of mines such as Wheal Towan and United Hills (Tywarnhayle).

"Porthtowan" appears to mean "sand-dune cove". Sand, of course, is very much in evidence: in winter storms often carry it well up the road; but why the reference to sand-dunes, which would suit Perranporth far better? The answer may be, as Padel suggests, that the cove takes its name from Towan Farm, on the high ground a little to the east. So then one might ask why the farm is so called...

1 **To begin the walk, either go back up the road, turning left and right at the top, or to avoid what can be quite heavy traffic in summer cross the bridge on the left just after you have passed the Post Office and other shops and walk beside the line of newish bungalows and houses, eventually emerging at the coast road opposite the Avalon Restaurant; you then turn right and immediately left. You should now be walking inland, up the canyon-like valley with its rushing stream.** Straight away on the left you will see the stack of an old mine building. This is a relic of the Echo Corner Shaft of South Wheal Towan.

SOUTH WHEAL TOWAN

This was a copper mine which sold ore to the value of nearly £118,000 between 1818 and 1847, but by 1870 was employing only eight people. Old photographs, such as the first one on page 30 in Clive Benney's first book, show twin stacks side by side here. A 40-inch pumping engine was installed, later to be replaced by a 70-inch. The cylinder bed stones from South Wheal Towan now belong to the museum at St Agnes, and are displayed outside. They are of special interest, because there are sets of bolt-holes for both the 40-inch and the 70-inch cylinders, suggesting that the engineers who installed the earlier engine anticipated the need for greater power later.

2 **Less than a hundred yards further on, go up the track on the left. (The fence is there to deter drivers and equestrians; gaps at the far end allow walkers through.) It leads to a ruined engine house with a separate stack beside it - relics of Tywarnhayle Mine. (Please note: this part of the walk is, strictly speaking, a diversion, and it involves some quite steep climbs, so you may prefer to continue up the road and follow the directions from point 3; but by doing so you will miss some of the most interesting and dramatically situated mining remains in Cornwall.)**

The engine house at Taylor's Shaft, thought to be one of the oldest surviving in Cornwall

TYWARNHAYLE MINE

For much of the information here and in the walk directions dealing with Tywarnhayle, I am indebted to an article by Dr Robin Smith of the Royal School of Mines. Copies may be available from Porthtowan post office.

Tywarnhale, Tywarnhaile or Tywarnhayle ("ti war an hayle", house on the estuary) is really the name of an ancient manor, but is used to refer to a group of copper mines whose workings were combined. Wheal Rock was working at least as far back as 1750. In 1809 it was bought by Andrew Vivian, who re-named it United Hills. He installed a "little puffing engine" with a 12-inch cylinder, made by his partner, Richard Trevithick. After heavy losses, the mine was closed in 1815. A new company re-opened it in 1826, installing a 58-inch engine bought from Lambo Mine, Gwinear, and later an 80-inch, previously at Wheal Towan. This period witnessed two serious accidents, both caused by bursting boilers. The first, in 1827, caused no deaths but showered bricks and other debris into the valley. On Wednesday 3rd February 1830, nine people were killed, including a boy and a girl, when a boiler which had only recently been repaired at Redruth Hammer Mill exploded, completely without warning. Seven of the victims had been warming themselves before starting work.

The mine was at its most prosperous in the late 1830s; between 1836 and 1850, the depth of the workings increased from 36 to 100 fathoms below adit, and in the period 1826-52, 67,462 tons of copper ore were raised, according to the surviving records. Further losses led to closure in 1852. A new attempt was made in 1859, but despite the report in the "Western Daily Mercury" of 26 March 1864, claiming that "there is little doubt that Tywarnhaile Mine will be one of the best copper mines in the country", this venture closed down later that same year (1864).

In 1906 yet another company began work here, concentrating on the copper still remaining in the surface dumps and the underground workings above the water-line, which was at the 40-fathom level. They erected the Power House by the road, and used coal brought from Portreath to manufacture gas, which in turn powered generators to supply electricity to the new pump at Taylor's Shaft. This was the first electrically driven Centrifugal Pumping System used in Cornwall, and it worked very well; even so, the company, to quote Dr Smith, "went into liquidation" in 1907, and therefore the lower mine workings inevitably followed suit. H.V. Williams' little book and also the St Agnes Museum Trust's Journal No.4 have a photograph of the electric pump being lowered into place beside the already roofless engine house. The same picture is in Clive Benney's 1850-1920 book, plus another giving a more general view of Tywarnhayle at that period. At the same time, one of the first Elmore oil vacuum plants for flotation (separation of ore from unwanted material by forming a froth to which the ore particles cling) was installed; the remains of this can be seen below the small stack by Monkton's Shaft at the corner, opposite Wheal Music - point 4 in the directions. The inventor, Mr Elmore, was a director of the company at the time.

From 1908, apart from a period during World War 2, Tywarnhayle was in use to train students of the Royal School of Mines, but the RSM terminated its lease late in the 1990s. Some information about the subsequent efforts by the local authority and the Carn Brea Mining Society to maintain underground access and to protect and make safe the surface remains is given in "Exploring Cornish Mines" Volume 5.

The engine house, probably part of the old Wheal Rock, is thought to be one of the oldest surviving in Cornwall. Its design is unique, and its engine, moved here some time after 1826, is said to have been the last one in Cornwall to use a wooden bob. Flat-rods were led from the bob kingpost through the rear window of the house to James' Shaft, on the higher ground. The trench is still visible on the hillside. WARNING: THE BUILDING IS IN AN ADVANCED STATE OF DECAY. PLEASE DO NOT ATTEMPT TO ENTER IT. The bob wall overlooks an impressive shaft known as Taylor's, full of cavernous drippings and the sound of rushing water; it is covered with a metal cage, but care is still needed if you walk around the edge, because the ground is far from stable in places. Beside Taylor's Shaft are the foundations for the electric pump used here in 1906-7, and for an electric hoist. The buildings below, beside the road, include what was formerly the Power House for generating the electricity.

Return the same way, but just before reaching the road take the path almost straight ahead which climbs quite steeply. After a sharp right turn you pass a small quarry, probably the source of much of the stone in the older mine buildings, and soon afterwards you will see below you a long, low, ruined building which is said to have been the mine's Count House. On the left of the path as you approach the fine engine house at John's (or Roberts') Shaft on the top of the hill are the remains of sorting floors where stones of copper were hand picked from the mined rock, and spalling floors where workers used heavy hammers to break down large lumps. Above them, in an area now overgrown with gorse

John's engine house, with a glimpse of the sea

and bracken, was a pond to store cooling water for some of the mine's steam engines. From the engine house you have a good view of several shafts on the other side of the valley, each surrounded by the material extracted when it was sunk; these were all unsuccessful trial borings, made in hopes of finding a continuation of the lode.

John's engine house contained a long-stroke 70-inch engine which later saw service at Wheal Uny, Redruth. Note the walled-in balance pit, which provided some shelter at this windy spot for the wooden balance bob.

Continue on the widish track leading towards a small building with a corrugated roof; inside are benches and a hearth. This hut stands by James' Shaft, which has a timber cover. **After passing the hut, take the track on the right,** and a few yards further on, just to the right of the track, is a little cutting leading to a mine portal; this was the access point for the pit railway. (Ore from the mine was hoisted to this point from the workings below, loaded into wagons, and taken by rail round the hill to dressing floors beside the road.) The gulley is rather overgrown, but you should have no great trouble walking along it. A timber framework prevents access to the shaft, but you can see quite far in and get some impression of underground workings. A little further on, beyond the boarded-up entrance to Gardiner's or Railway Shaft, the main track is blocked by a pile of rubble near Gardiner's Engine Shaft, where there was once an engine house for an 80-inch pumping engine, later replaced by a 70-inch one; the stack on the scree slope below belonged to a copper crusher which formerly stood beside the cottages below. By the track down there is the sewage farm, and further away, to the right, was the deep pit created by Wheal Music; when I researched this book originally in 1989 it was partially filled with sludge brought here from Wheal Concord, and by 1993 it had totally disappeared, the level surface of the infilling material now grassed over and looking like any other field.

Return from here to where the tracks divided, near the hut. The track bearing right leads back towards Porthtowan, so ignore this and turn left, returning by the same route past John's engine house and back down to the valley road.

WHEAL MUSIC

Despite its attractive name, in its early years Wheal Music had a grim reputation for serious accidents. The best-known relic of this mine was the "Navvy Pit". The copper here was mined down to about 300 feet, but at higher levels the lodes were, to quote George Henwood, "split up into minute strings and branches, none of which were singly worth pursuit. The whole rock was then removed and the copper ores extracted. An excavation of an elliptical form of about an acre in area and 25 fathoms in depth stands open to the day."

The Navvy Pit in 1989, almost completely filled in with rubbish and mine waste. John's engine house on the ridge.

(Henwood was writing in the middle of the 19th century.) All this openwork (or "stockwork") mining seems to have been done before 1833, and one early commentator stated that profits of £100,000 were made. During recent years the impressive cavity became a receptacle for rubbish, so the decision in the early 1980s to dump waste from Wheal Concord in it was regarded by many as an improvement, even though the obliteration of so notable a feature of the mining landscape is regrettable. (The modern Wheal Concord, formed in 1980 to explore for tin on the site of an old mine of the same name west of Blackwater, closed in 1985 as a result of the sudden fall in tin prices.)

3 Turn left on the valley road, passing the Power House and other former mine buildings. Notice that the banks of the stream here are lined with walls; this is because the valley-floor level has been raised several feet by deposits of rubble from the mine. Retaining walls have been built in several places up on the left to hold the huge burrows in place. In the yard just past the Power House is a wooden trap-door; this is one route by which the students entered the shallower mine workings; the deeper ones are all flooded. The trap-door provides access to the Tywarnhayle adit, which flows under the road to join the stream, so the students had to wade.

4 Just before the road bends right, notice on your left the ruins of the Elmore separation plant. To continue the walk, turn left immediately

beyond that; but first it is worth going over to the right to inspect the engine house of Wheal Ellen, with its castellated stack. This never had an engine in it: it was built for a long-stroke Harvey 70-inch engine from Boscawen Mine (near Scorrier), but the cash ran out before it was moved and it ended up at a mine in mid-Wales!

WHEAL ELLEN

This copper mine was also sometimes known as Old Basset Mine, not to be confused with the great Basset mines south of Carn Brea, although the name here, as there, presumably alludes to the great landowning family of Tehidy. Wheal Ellen worked mainly between 1826 and 1862, producing about 24,000 tons of copper ore. According to J.H.Collins, it "re-opened about 1907 for complex zinc-copper ores, but did not continue long." Some if not all of the concrete foundations and buildings near the engine house are relics of that period. Also nearby are much older structures - wheelpits and what look like calciners among them.

Like a small castle, Wheal Ellen guards the entrance to the Porthtowan valley, while the engine house at John's Shaft stands sentinel above.

Now walk up the side-valley going north-east; take the main track, not the one starting at a gateway on the right, and ignore the track going up on the left a few yards later. As is obvious because of all the old dumps and shafts on both sides of the stream, there were several small mines in this area. The cobbled surface of the track probably indicates that it used to serve these mines. They included Wheal Charles on the southern edge of Tywarnhayle; down beside the stream, Wheal Fancy and East Fancy, which produced tin; and Prince Royal further east, a copper mine. Wheal Fancy and Prince Royal were worked together under the name East Tywarnhayle by a company formed in 1864. After the sewage works, notice the shafts on the right.

Soon you have to cross the stream: some wading or a jump may be necessary, but a plank on the right side provided a handy footbridge when I was last there. The path continues by the stream along what the locals call "shady walk". Certainly it is sheltered, if not often literally shady, and makes a delightful contrast to the exposed cliffs. As it is a bridleway, you may well encounter mud, but at the worst patch you can avoid it by walking on top of the bank to your left. A stone footbridge marks the start of a pretty footpath (not part of the route I am recommending here) which climbs through woodland to Trevissick Farm; from there the map shows it continuing to the road, but I haven't explored that end of it. Where the path divides, go either way, but I like the lower path better, which keeps close to the stream and surprisingly is rather less muddy than the upper one. Just before Banns Farm, flowing in from the right is water emerging from a small tunnel, an adit which appears to have belonged to a small mine called Wheal Banns, or possibly to Prince Royal Mine, mentioned above, or Trenethick Mine, another copper mine a little further east. According to Dines there are no records of output from Wheal Banns, but Collins mentions "small sales of tin ore about the year 1881". You are now coming into Banns Vale.

5 At the road, turn left, and continue on the road for about half a mile. "Banns" means "hollow", and as you struggle up the hill on the far side you understand why the settlement is so called! At the top you have a good view of St Agnes Beacon ahead, with the engine houses of Wheal Coates on the skyline to its left; and much further left - almost behind you, in fact - is Carn Brea. At the T-junction, go straight across on to the path (signposted to Mingoose and St Agnes, though the sign is now virtually illegible). At the cottages, keep to the path on the right. Cross the stream by stepping-stones, and after the stile go diagonally to your right over the field: look for a stone stile with a small metal gate tied in place on the far side. Having negotiated these, keep near the hedge on your left; this will bring you to another gate-plus-stile and a road.

6 Turn left, and at the T-junction, by the attractively converted chapel, left again. You now pass through the pretty village of Mingoose (from the Cornish, "edge of the wood"). Near the valley-bottom is the former inn, the Miners Arms, which seems to have ceased business by 1880.

7 A few yards later, take the signed public footpath on the right. (But if you're in need of refreshments, continue up to the main road - under half a mile - where you will find the Victory Inn.) **Keep to the main path down the valley.** After about half a mile, notice the evidence of mining on the far (east) side of the valley.

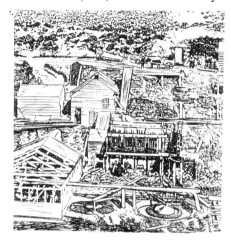

Left: My sketch is based on one of several photos taken in about 1912 of a small mine, Wheal Charlotte, on the east side of the valley. The concrete bases of the two buddles, together with slight remains of walls and buildings, still lurk amid the scrub.

Below: the ruins of the building which once housed Charlotte United mine's 30-inch pumping engine

The hillside on the left, too, is riddled with shafts: at least ten are marked by warning posts all around the spoil heaps on the hilltop, and it is easy enough to walk through the low gorse and heather to see them... but this is obviously the kind of area where wary walking is essential: please remember that old shafts whose existence has been forgotten sometimes suddenly reveal themselves in areas like this. As you continue along the main path near the stream you will see many more shafts on both sides. After you have passed the engine house of Charlotte United mine, built for a 30-inch pumping engine, the path comes down close to the stream.

8 **Take the wide track up the hillside to the left; a post with acorn signs stands at the foot of it.**

(Alternatively, go down to the cove first. Refreshments are usually available at the National Trust car park in summer, and often even out of season, usually on Sundays. The site of the car park was once covered with mine buildings. A large waterwheel driving stamps once occupied the structure overlooking the toilets; the tailrace opening can still be seen, as well as the leat and dam further up the valley which supplied it. In the cliffs on the left are the mouths of two adits from Great Wheal Charlotte; on the right are two linked caves, known locally as "Two Vuggs". The right-hand one appears to have an adit opening at the far end, and the other has a "blow-hole": this is the hole associated in legend with the Giant Bolster... See the note on St Agnes and its Church (pages 77-8). If the tide is low enough - and, preferably, still going out - you may wish to walk along the beach on the right to explore the cave beneath Wheal Coates: see pages 94 and 96. From the car park, you could cross the lower footbridge and go up the narrow path round the cliff-edge to continue the walk, if you have a good head for heights, or return up the valley and take the wide track I have mentioned.)

You are now on the coastal footpath, and don't need any further directions in order to find Porthtowan and your car.

However, I should point out that the large area of mine waste which you cross almost at once, as soon as you have passed the headland on the south of Chapel Porth, was created by Great Wheal Charlotte, and even though only the bob wall remains of its engine house, it is worth taking the path on the left to see it, looking now like a triumphal arch - or perhaps a monument to the memory of Cornish mining. The surviving records refer only to the period from 1834 to 1840, when just under 3,000 tons of copper were produced; but the records must be very incomplete, to judge by the devastation this mine caused along a large stretch of fine cliff.

Photo by Simon V. Jones

WALK 10

As you approach Porthtowan, you are in the area exploited by Wheal Towan, an important copper mine, but most of the evidence of its activities is further inland, near the road.

WHEAL TOWAN

A. K. Hamilton Jenkin tells in detail the story of Ralph Allen Daniell's faith in the prospects of this mine at the start of the 19th century. Eventually he was repaid with such handsome profits that he was nicknamed "Guinea-a-Minute Daniell". See the note on John Opie on page 65. The same nickname was given at about the same time to the owner of Wheal Neptune and other mines near Marazion: see "Mines and Miners of Cornwall" Volume 4.

Beside the beach on the south side at Porthtowan, a dwelling, formerly a café (as shown in the photograph on page 119), has been created from an old engine house: this was built in 1872 and belonged to New Wheal Towan, a small mine whose workings connected with those of Wheal Lushington, which was up on the cliff. Like the Wheal Ellen engine house, this building never had an engine in it. A rotative beam engine from Ireland was landed at Penryn and reached the site but was never erected. It was to have worked pumps underground by means of flat-rods going through the adit still visible behind. The bungalow next to New Wheal Towan engine house was originally of wood and was the former count house of Great Wheal Charlotte, taken down and re-erected as a dwelling. Bricks from the upper part of the engine house stack were used for the foundations.

For a more detailed account of the history of New Wheal Towan by Kenneth Brown, see the most recent Journal of the St Agnes Museum Trust, No. 15. The same issue contains Ron and Rose Trengove's interesting and well illustrated story of the work carried out to consolidate and refurbish the engine house between 1991 and 1993.

WALK 11
PORTREATH, THE OLD TRAMROAD, PORTHTOWAN & THE CLIFFS
About 8½ miles, or about 7 if Porthtowan is omitted

Map for Walks 11, 14 &15

① to 5 Walk 11
① to ⑤ Walk 14
❶ to ❼ Walk 15

© Crown Copyright and/or database right. All rights reserved. Licence number 100024943.

© Crown Copyright

NOTE: WALKS 11-15

These 5 walks based on Portreath were all included in *Exploring Cornwall's Tramway Trails* Volume 2 (1997, revised second edition 2000). The directions have, where necessary, been updated for this book, but for detailed information about the fascinating history of this area you need the earlier book.

WALK 11

Including a lunch-stop of nearly an hour in Porthtowan, we spent about five hours on this walk, taking it at a leisurely pace, and felt at the end that we'd had a splendid day out. About half of the inland part is along the trackbed of the Portreath Tramroad (the early mineral railway: see the note on Portreath), which means level walking. At Cambrose the walk route leaves the Tramroad and follows quiet country roads with superb inland views. Porthtowan is worth visiting, whether for its fine surfing beach, its pub/café refreshments, or its industrial-archaeological interest; but if you prefer you can shorten the walk by cutting across to the cliffs west of the village. The coast path between Porthtowan and Portreath offers dramatic cliff scenery plus views back to St Agnes Head and forward to Godrevy lighthouse and St Ives Bay. Most of this section is fairly level, but there are two steep descents and climbs; steps have been cut to make the going easier. Just inland is a former airfield, now a Ministry of Defence establishment; under the terms of the Official Secrets Act it has to be surrounded by a high fence, and for nearly two miles the coast path runs beside that. Luckily, it's fairly unobtrusive most of the time.

You are unlikely to need waterproof footwear except perhaps early in the walk, on parts of the old railway. Shops and toilets are available in Portreath and Porthtowan, and there are several pubs along the way, at Portreath, Porthtowan and Bridge.

Two little books - now, unfortunately, hard to find - give fascinating details about the history of this area, namely *Portreath: Some Chapters in its History* by Michael Tangye (1968) and *Memories of Nancekuke* by Ernest Landry (1978).

Directions are given from the main car park overlooking the beach at Portreath.

PORTREATH

The name means "sandy bay" or "sandy harbour". Traces of a harbour on the western side of the cove have been found. They date back at least to the early 18th century and possibly to the 16th, but the present harbour was built between 1760 and 1860. Welsh coal and timber were imported, and the chief export was copper ore for smelting in South Wales. Between 1809 and 1818 a horse-drawn railway, the Portreath Tramroad, was built to serve the mines, chiefly those around Scorrier and St Day, but by the 1830s much of the tramroad's business was being taken by the Redruth & Chasewater Railway, another horse-drawn system, which served the port of Devoran on the south coast. When a branch of the Hayle Railway was extended to Portreath late in the 1830s via a steep incline things improved for a while, but the decline of the copper mines and the conversion of the R & C Railway to steam traction during the 1850s hit Portreath hard. The voyage between South Wales and south-coast ports like Devoran and Penryn was long and dangerous, but Portreath's harbour, like those at Newquay and St Agnes, was too exposed to be used safely in rough weather. The many attempts to protect ships in Portreath harbour from heavy seas were not very successful; nevertheless, between the 1850s and the 1920s the port was used by a fleet of small steam colliers owned by the Hain family. Shipbuilding flourished here in the 1860s and '70s, and so did seine fishing until the disappearance of the pilchard shoals early in the 20th century. Interesting photographs of Portreath in the late 19th and early 20th centuries are in L.J.Bullen's Volume 4. (See Further Reading.)

The entrance to the inner harbour
Photo: Simon V Jones

1 Begin the walk by following the directions in section 1 of Walk 13. Don't take the left turning, but continue past the Portreath Arms and then take the side road on the left, Sunnyvale Road, which follows the course of the Tramroad. Sunnyvale Road eventually rejoins the main road, but a few yards before that take the footpath on the left, still following the Tramroad track. Watch out as you go for lines of exposed "setts" (granite sleeper-blocks), some of which still feature the remains of the iron spikes that held down the plates. **Continue ahead across the minor road leading to RAF Portreath.** As the path approaches the small village of Bridge, a side path leads down to the Bridge Inn. If you don't need a refreshment stop yet, continue along the Tramroad path, past the cottage named Hillside; there keep right, ignoring the uphill track. On this stretch you will see a particularly well-preserved group of setts, at one of the passing loops which were constructed every half-mile along the Tramroad. **The next small settlement is Cambrose. Still continue ahead there, bearing left just beyond the small row of cottages. This brings you to a minor road, with Carn View Cottage opposite.**

2 Turn left on the minor road. Ignore the left turning soon after; continue uphill, with the view to the right and ahead steadily widening out till finally it includes St Agnes Beacon as well as Carn Brea. The mine stack among the houses of Redruth just left of Carn Brea is Pednandrea (when it was built in 1824, the tallest mine chimney in Cornwall at 145 feet; the brick-built top half has been demolished, but even now it dominates the town); left of that in the distance is Carn Marth, a taller hill than Carn Brea; then the triple engine houses of Wheal Peevor; next Hallenbeagle, two engine houses - one of them now little more than a stack - beside the main railway line and the A30; further left again, Doctor's Shaft, North Treskerby. **The road turns right, left and right again.**

3 A few hundred yards past the second right bend, take the left turning past several houses and farm buildings. Turn left at the T-junction, beside the entrance to School Farm.

Before the hamlets of Great and Little Nancekuke were destroyed in 1939, the young children from there and other nearby settlements attended a Board Day School close to this farm. In the 1890s, when Ernest Landry attended it, it had two lady teachers and 60-70 pupils.

Now on your right you have what was once Nancekuke Common, and on your left a disused airfield, now "a prohibited place within the meaning of the Official Secrets Act", as the notice at the entrance puts it. (See the note later on Nancekuke Defence Area.) **Follow the road round, and now you are heading towards St Agnes Beacon. On the left are the buildings of Factory Farm.**

The name comes from the gunpowder factory which was once at the seaward end of Factory Lane; it closed down in 1862 after an explosion.

Not far past that is Factory Lane, a wide track leading straight to the coast, and this is the way to go if you don't want to include Porthtowan on your walk - but you'll miss some impressive cliff scenery, too. Otherwise, continue along the road as it gradually descends to the outskirts of the village.

4 Here you have a choice of routes into Porthtowan. (A) is probably a little shorter and passes a group of shops, but (B) is more attractive and avoids any walking on a road that can be busy in summer.

(A) Go down to the main road and turn left. A short way along, to reduce the road walking you could take a path on the right - sometimes rather overgrown - which passes through the Rosehill Park caravan site and returns you to the road near the bottom of the hill. From there you could walk down the side-road on the left into Porthtowan, or continue ahead as far as the Avalon Tea Room & Restaurant and take the footpath opposite, which starts on the right side of the petrol station and ends by crossing the bridge almost opposite the shops.

(B) Just before the main road, turn left up the steepish tarmacked lane among houses and bear left, continuing uphill on a track which passes South View Farm and West Towan House. On the right now is an area riddled with mine workings. Soon you reach the coast path; bear right for Porthtowan.

At the headland on the south side you have a good view over the splendid surfing beach and the holiday developments, many of them very tatty and flimsy, others looking like a rather half-hearted attempt to emulate the Costa del Sol. A few old cottages and Victorian or Edwardian villas remain; and notice, close at hand below you as you walk down, an engine house (though in fact no engine was ever installed in it), with a truncated castellated chimney.

NEW WHEAL TOWAN

The engine house dates from 1872, when New Wheal Towan was established with the aim of retrying old workings of a mine called Wheal Lushington in the hill behind. An old adit runs from behind the engine house and emerges at the foot of the cliffs, and the plan was to run flat-rods through this adit to work pumps - but nothing came of the scheme. An engine arrived from Ireland (via Penryn!) but merely lay on the ground before it was eventually broken up. After some years in use as a café (see the photograph on the next page), the building was splendidly restored

WALK 11

to its original appearance and is now a private house. The bungalow next door (on the seaward side) is built around a wooden structure which was the relocated count house of Wheal Charlotte, worked early this century near Chapel Porth. Foundations for it were made using the brick upper part of the New Wheal Towan stack.

For a note about Porthtowan, see pages 102-3.

5 To return to Portreath, follow the coast path sign close to the Unicorn - retracing your footsteps, if you came by route (B).

From now on, directions would be superfluous - but you may be glad to have a few details pointed out.

At first there are many capped shafts of old mine workings. Several small mines exploited this area at different times, extracting mainly copper, but also some tin, lead, iron, zinc and silver; their adits (drainage shafts) opened on to the cliff face. Ernest Landry writes about an adit from West Wheal Towan which led out to a big cave where seals used to breed: "I used to take visitors to the farm (i.e. Factory Farm) down the mine shaft which was fitted with ladders ... to this tunnel to the sea ... It was a marvellous sight at the end of this tunnel watching the mother seals coming into the cave on the incoming tide to nurse their young ones." These cliffs are very unstable, as the warning notices emphasise. The large rock at the southern end of Porthtowan beach, for example, was once joined to the mainland near the top: a picture of it as it was is on the cover of Landry's book. In that form, its name, the Tobban Horse, is perhaps more understandable. The top of the huge natural arch later collapsed, obscuring many old mine workings in the cliffs below. ("Tobban" means "mound" or "bank", and probably refers to a nearby field.) The cliffs between Tobban Horse and Sally Point, about half a mile further on, were, says Landry, "the last place where the Cornish Chough was seen in this district".

Soon you approach the fence of RAF Portreath, otherwise known as the Nancekuke Defence Area.

WALK 11
NANCEKUKE

Nancekuke was part of the Tehidy Estate. When the estate broke up, in 1916, most of the Nancekuke tenant farmers took out mortgages to buy their own farms, and then proceeded to improve them greatly. "I remember the spring of 1939," writes Landry. "It had every prospect of being a good season. All the farms on Nancekuke were a picture to look at, well-farmed by a good lot of hard-working, contented farmers."

Then the authorities announced that the area was required by the RAF as an airfield, and a Minister came down to tell the farmers that everyone had to make sacrifices during wartime. "I remember the sacrifice this Minister made sometime after was a higher position in the Government." The bitterness of Landry's account of this takeover is understandable in view of the Minister's promise that the farms would be restored to their former owners after the war, because when that time came the Ministry of Supply took the area over and added more land to it, including five acres of Factory Farm, then surrounded it with a tall fence and built, in Landry's words, "a poison factory on this lovely part of Cornwall, a disgrace and eye-sore to any country in peace-time."

Just what was produced or investigated in that building remained secret, but rumours abounded of seals dying mysteriously nearby, and several employees became ill and claimed compensation; only after many years was the justice of their claim finally recognised. John Branfield's novel for teenagers, "Nancekuke", is based on these events. In recent times it has emerged that twenty tons of the deadly nerve agent Sarin was among the products of Nancekuke Chemical Defence Establishment.

The CDE was decommissioned between 1976 and 1980, when the work was transferred to Porton Down in Wiltshire. A cleaning-up programme was carried out then, but doubts have persisted about poisonous substances that might still remain, and further "remediation" work is due to start in 2005. Some re-routing of the coast path may follow.

The site is now part of the Early Warning System, scanning the Atlantic by radar; the big "radome sphere", designed to protect the radar installations, is a recent feature. I'm sorry the fence is still considered necessary; at least it is less tall and ugly than before.

The name, Nancekuke, by the way, appears to mean "hollow valley" or possibly "empty, worthless valley"; food for thought there, perhaps.

Just before the fence begins there are a small concrete reservoir and a concrete chimney with a long brick-lined flue leading up to it from the foundations of a boiler house, and below, a shaft covered by an enormous concrete cap crowned with a "bat castle". Around the shaft are somewhat older concrete structures, some of them the bases for horizontal pumping and winding engines, others the remains of settling tanks. The truncated rectangular wall near the shaft is what survives of the count house. The shaft is called Vivian's (or Ladder) Shaft and belonged to an old mine called Wheal Tye. It was one of many small mines which became part of West Wheal Towan, and this may well be the shaft "fitted with ladders" that Ernest Landry used to take his visitors down. The shaft was reopened in 1927; as Dines puts it, "no development ensued," but the stack and other ruins may date from then, or from the period 1920-5 when an enterprise named Sally Bottoms was reworking sections of several old mines in this area.

"Sally Bottom" itself is the next cove, otherwise called Kerriack or Cayack Cove. Before descending to it you walk through a flat-rod trench dating from around the middle of the 19th century; the concrete shelters in it were used in World War 2 and were associated with a target for aircraft gunnery practice on the cliff nearby. As you go down to the cove, care is needed if you use the lower group of steps, because much of the soil around the vertical wooden boards has been eroded. At the bottom, notice the fenced shaft and the ancient-looking ruins of mine buildings to the left, inside the MOD perimeter fence. The site of a stamps engine can be seen. The other ruins, close to the path just after it has crossed the second little stream, are the remains of rifle butts.

Ernest Landry tells the story of Sally Peters, who was born in a thatched cottage in the valley above the cove now named after her. Both her parents were engaged in tin mining or streaming there - presumably during the late 18th or early 19th century - and she too worked as a bal maiden (breaking up ore before it was fed to the stamps machine) when young, but later married a French sailor and lived for a time at St Nazaire. She returned to her native valley, though, after many adventures and personal tragedies, and in old age became a local legend through the help she gave to the sick and aged, many of whom she saved from being consigned to the workhouse.

The valley and nearby cliffs had been mined for centuries, and tin streaming was carried out at the seaward end. Water was constantly

*Remains of rifle butts at Sally Bottom,
photographed in 1996*

required there to operate the waterwheels which drove the stamps and buddles, and for the other dressing processes, so the valley was dammed to create a reservoir "of quite half an acre in extent", says Landry; the small reservoir you see as you descend probably occupies part of the same site. The old mine in the valley was called Wheal Sally. In the 1920s shafts were sunk there by the Sally Bottoms company, seeking lead and zinc.

Sally Bay was once famous for its limpets and winkles; Landry tells of the old soldier with a wooden leg who used to scale the precipitous path or staircase down to the beach once a week and sell the cooked limpets, with salt, pepper and vinegar to taste, in the street near Redruth town clock. As you go up the steps on the far side, look back to see the small waterfall - except perhaps during a dry summer.

The next cove, with very sheer cliffs and a cave, is called Gollyn, Gullan or Gullyn Cove; Gullyn is also the name of the rocky island there.

Later there are more steps into a valley named Hayle Ulla. "Hayle" here probably refers to marshy ground. Look back to see the island-rock called the Diamond ... one name that doesn't require an explanation. Near the kissing-gate, the fence ends at last. Next comes Gooden Heane Point; whatever the name means, it's well worth going out to the farthest tip for the view of the cove and beach, with a glimpse of the white landmark at Portreath ahead and Godrevy beyond.

The landmark (or "daymark", since it contains no light), was built about 1800 and doubled as navigational aid and coastguards' and pilots' lookout; the entrance, though sealed now, is still clearly visible. Its local nicknames are "The Pepperpot" and "The Lighthouse". The latter name, like the former, perhaps simply alludes to its appearance, but it is said that a signal light used to be shone from it. A small plaque attached to the building in 1995 states that Laurence Binyon wrote "Hymn to the Fallen" ("They shall not grow old ...") "on this spot". On the way down into Portreath you will pass a rather quaint little brick-built castellated "summer house" or "watchtower"; according to another source, it was here the poet wrote his famous lines. Yet others say that he wrote them at Polzeath, near Padstow. Take your pick! (Polzeath - Portreath... was the poet's hand-writing to blame for the confusion?)

Next you have an excellent view in turn of the long jetty and the outer and inner basins of the harbour. At the end of the pier (known locally as "Monkey Island") is a small round building, "The Monkey House"; it was built to protect men on lookout duty some years after the jetty was extended in 1824. The jetty is very dangerous to walk along in rough weather, and is therefore closed to the public.

Just after passing the house called Fairwinds, you could take the path sharp right, leading down to the harbour, and walk round to the far side and past the Waterfront pub back to the car park. If you do go down to the north side of the harbour, notice the small round building at the top of a flight of steps at the seaward end. Officially the Lower Coastguards' (or Pilots') Lookout, this was, says Michael Tangye, "used as a mortuary for wreck victims and others" and is still called "Deadman's Hut".

WALK 12
THE FIRST OF TWO SHORT WALKS AT PORTREATH:
THE WESTERN CLIFFS, GREEN LANE & FEADON

About 3 miles, or can be split into walks of about 1 & 2 miles

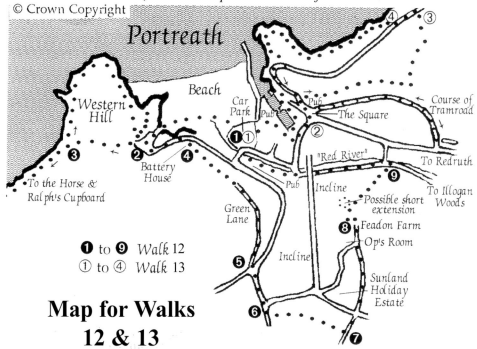

© Crown Copyright

© Crown Copyright and/or database right. All rights reserved. Licence number 100024943.

Both these little walks give excellent bird's-eye views of the village and harbour plus stunning cliff scenery. By the same token, both involve a fair bit of uphill walking.

The suggested extension to this first walk gives one of the best views of Portreath, plus some very pleasant country walking. The cliff-edge path around Western Hill might be unsuitable for anyone who suffers from vertigo, but there are other paths that run a bit further inland. As you descend from the cliffs there is a very steep section where you really need shoes or boots with a good grip, or a walking stick, or both. Mud could be a bit of a problem near Feadon Farm.

The start/end point is the main car park overlooking Portreath beach.

See the note about Walks 11-15, at the start of Walk 11.

WALK 12

1 If the tide allows, start by crossing to the far (western) side of the beach. (If not, follow the directions in brackets below.)
Notice the old mine workings in the cliffs beneath Battery House. If you go into the small cave and look up you will see a good example of the way miners exploited mineral lodes that were exposed on a cliff face. The beach itself was a rich source of tin, deposited in the sand by the "Red River", which flowed from the heart of the mining country, and even by the little stream that reaches the beach on the far (west) side. Gold as well as tin was recovered from that stream.
Go up the slipway and lane to Smugglers' Cottage.
(If the tide is too high, use instead Battery Hill, the minor road that runs close to the cliff edge and passes Battery House: detailson pages 141-2. This would also be the better way to go if you want to do only the inland part of this walk; for that, take the path that cuts back sharply just before you reach Battery House, and follow the directions from section 4, line 4, page 127.)

2 From Smugglers' Cottage take the path running up the sheltered little valley, signed North Coast Foot Path. Ignore the small path up on the right beside the National Trust Western Hill sign.
Western Hill's old name, Tregea Hill, is, suggested Charles Henderson, a corruption of "Tregear", and "gear" or "ker" in Cornish place-names indicates a fort, so the hill and headland are likely to have been the site of one of the many early "cliff castles".
Near the top, two more paths go off towards the cliff edge, and you could use either of them if you want the shortest route, but I'd recommend you to go on up to the top.

3 On reaching the cliff edge there, if you enjoy dramatic cliff scenery I suggest that you first continue ahead for about 250m to get the best view of the rocky promontory known as The Horse, and the gulley beyond, called Ralph's Cupboard (photo overleaf). The latter is thought by some to have been named after a smuggler who allegedly stored his contraband there; others say that the name refers to an ancient legendary giant called Wrath. **Then retrace your steps and take the narrow path which runs most of the way around the seaward side of Western Hill - or choose one of the other paths running a little further inland if you'd prefer.** Naturally, the path nearest the edge gives the best views, first of the small island called Gull Rock and later of Portreath and the coast

125

Looking down on the Horse and Ralph's Cupboard from the cliff edge

north-east. When you come to a wide, grassy area you have what I think is the best of all views of Portreath. The Incline for the Hayle Railway and the route of the Tramroad are both clearly seen. **The best way down is via the steep slope that heads towards the bungalow in the valley; particular care not to slip is needed on the grassy first section, but later there are some helpful steps.**

Just before you reach the bottom of the slope, you might care to walk a short way along the side path going up on the left. This soon leads to a lower path which runs immediately above the site of Portreath's original small harbour (1713). As at St Agnes, storms soon destroyed it. (There is more about Portreath's early harbour on page 141.) If you look right you may be able to make out what could be the remains of a wider track running up to this point from just behind Smugglers' Cottage, and this may be the route by which goods was conveyed to and from ships tied up at the quay.

Return the same way and go on down to the valley close to Smugglers' Cottage. Continuing via the road above takes you past Battery House. Here in 1782 a battery of cannons was set up to protect the cove from attacks by privateers and the French. Again see page 141 for more about this and Smugglers' Cottage.

4 You could simply return to the car park, or make a recommended extension of the walk by taking the uphill path which starts immediately beyond Battery House, and looks at first like a private entrance to another house, West-A-Way. The path turns sharp-right, up steps, giving you a close-up view of the small battlemented walls above Battery House. Another sharp turn, this time to the left, soon takes you to Green Lane - a good place to linger, for the fine view over the village. The lane becomes a minor road passing beside bungalows.

J.C.Burrow's 1895 photograph of the view from the Green Lane area

5 At the road junction go straight on. This is quite a busy road; walk facing the oncoming traffic. Ignore the two side roads on the left.

6 Less than 50m. beyond the second side road, turn left on to the signed public footpath, starting with a granite cattle-grid (a "Cornish stile"). The path runs beside the hedge on the right, crosses another stone grid at the corner, and continues in the same line across the next field to a wooden kissing-gate beside a farm gate.

7 Turn left along the farm lane (often extremely muddy, I'm afraid), and on reaching the buildings at Feadon Farm follow the footpath signs, turning first left, then right at the start of a concrete road.

Feadon (pronounced "Faydon") Farm belongs to the Duchy College and is used to give practical experience to students of agriculture.

At the corner you can see, to the left, the long, low, flat-roofed building still known as the Op's Room, built in 1941 as a control centre for operations associated with the nearby Portreath Airfield, on the other side of the valley at Nancekuke. In recent years it has been converted for use as a pub, but is now a private residence.

8 At the farmyard entrance turn left on to a narrow path, following a public footpath sign. The path turns right, and then another clearly signed path leads off, sharp-left, down into the wooded valley. Take this path, soon passing a small pond on your left.

When you come to a short length of wooden fence on your left (the remains of a stile), you could make an attractive short extension to the walk. For this, cross the fence and go over the footbridge. The path now runs uphill. A few steps plus a stone stile bring you to a picnic table and a good view over Portreath to the harbour and sea. The rest of the circular woodland path is uncomfortably steep at first, and has become rather overgrown, so I suggest you return the same way to the main path.

Continue downhill, soon joining a surfaced lane at the mock-military "Glenfeadon Castle". Go on down to Primrose Lane.

9 Turn left on that. Soon you pass the Glenfeadon House Hotel, with its impressive Georgian frontage. Glenfeadon House stands on the former site of the Portreath Tin Smelting House, founded in 1814. Records indicate that the smelter was busy and profitable, but it closed after only eleven years when its owners went into partnership with a larger firm. Large lumps of black clinker, said to be from the smelter, are on either side of the steps leading up to the main entrance of the hotel.

Continue under the bridge through the Incline. The Incline was cut through solid rock in 1837-8 as part of the Hayle Railway, which linked the Camborne and Redruth mines to the ports of Hayle and Portreath. A stationary engine at the top hauled wagons (laden mostly with coal) up from the harbour and lowered them (laden mostly with copper ore for shipment to South Wales for smelting). The line closed in 1932. See pages 133-4 for more about the Incline.

Go straight on along Tregea Terrace, with the small stream that was once one of Cornwall's "Red Rivers" on your right. After passing the Basset Arms, the path climbs to the road. Almost opposite the point where you come to the road, once stood the Portreath Tin Streaming Plant, dating from 1887. Located just the other side of the road bridge, close to the site now occupied by the "Beach Shop 'n' Surf", it employed a waterwheel and a steam engine to drive stamps and buddles. When the streaming plant closed I do not know - probably not later than 1933, when, to prevent the sea from continuing to be discoloured by mine waste at Portreath, the Red River was diverted underground to reach the sea further north. See page 137 for more on this.

Turn right for the car park.

The Incline in its working days
This copy of an old postcard seems to have been taken
from a cracked glass-plate negative.

WALK 13
THE SECOND SHORT WALK AT PORTREATH:
THE EASTERN CLIFFS
About 1½ miles
The map for this walk is on page 124.

The comments in the first paragraph at the start of Walk 12 apply to this one too, but unless you have a severe problem with heights you are unlikely to be worried by anything on this walk. The start/end point is again the main car park overlooking Portreath beach.

See the note about Walks 11-15, again on page 114.

1 From the car park take the pedestrian exit on the east side (right as you face the sea). Steps go down to a small sandy beach, part of what was once a slipway for launching newly-built ships. Walk straight ahead beside a row of modern houses and then left past the entrance to the Waterfront Inn. This stands on the site of the old "Fish Palace", where pilchards were salted, pressed and packed. From beside the pub you have a good view of the outer harbour basin. On the far side was the terminus of the Portreath Tramroad, the first railway to be laid above ground in Cornwall. Work started on it in 1809, and by 1819 it was completed as far as Poldice Mine, near St Day. The gauge was about three feet, and horses drew the wagons. The exact date of its closure is uncertain - probably before 1890.

The area you are walking through was formerly occupied by sheds, workshops, a double lime kiln, heaps of coal and limestone, and the various sidings and turntables belonging to the Hayle Railway. The old photograph on the opposite page gives some idea of how much it has changed during the past century-or-so. In the background can be seen the foot of the Incline.

Continuing inland, after passing a few more houses turn left to walk beside the inner harbour basin, then left again at the main road, which now turns right as it passes a group of shops on the right and the Portreath Arms on the left.

2 There (before coming to the pub) turn sharp-left on to the minor road, Lighthouse Hill, which runs above the north side of the harbour and climbs towards the cliffs. (The road's name refers to the so-called "Pepperpot" daymark tower, which doubled as a look-out. A flag-

signalling system was operated from it, but as far as I know it was never a lighthouse, although it may at some stage have had a lantern.) **Pass the pretty row of old cottages on your left, but just before the path that leads down to the harbour turn sharp-right up a steepish path, known as New Walk, with steps and railings.**

As you climb you get an excellent overview of the landward part of Portreath. In particular it's very obvious from here how the modern housing in the flat valley-bottom has replaced the various railway sidings, coal yards, fish cellar, lime kiln and other paraphernalia of a working port serving an industrial hinterland. On the opposite side of the valley is the Incline, now partially overgrown, which linked Portreath to the rest of the Hayle Railway. As you climb ever higher, the view extends ahead to the deep valley leading towards Redruth, along which ran Portreath's earlier mineral railway, known locally as the Tram, and on the skyline can be glimpsed Carn Marth and Carn Brea, at the centre of the region which both the railways and the port served.

Eventually the path bends left and begins to level off, and now for a short while there's little to see apart from the long fence and some of the buildings of RAF Portreath, otherwise known as the Nancekuke Defence Area (details on page 120). **Keep to the main path where it turns left again, ignoring a side path on the right.**

131

3 **Turn left at the road, passing a group of ugly concrete buildings, survivors of World War 2.** The view ahead, in contrast, is splendid, stretching along the coast to Godrevy Lighthouse and beyond to the hills above St Ives and Carbis Bay. **After about 80m turn right to find the Coastal Footpath.**

4 **Turn left on that. The rest of the way back to the car park, including a visit to the north side of the harbour, is described in the last four paragraphs of Walk 11 (pages 122-3).**

On the way, you will pass the "Pepperpot".

WALK 14
PORTREATH, ILLOGAN WOODS, ILLOGAN
CHURCH TOWN, BRIDGE & THE TRAMWAY
Just over 3 miles (5km)
The sketch map for this route is at the start of Walk 11.

This is a very easy walk with many attractive and interesting features: beautiful woodland, pleasant countryside with long views, and the oldest and prettiest part of Illogan village are the main but far from the only ones. The route passes two of Portreath's pubs; in addition there is a general store at Illogan Churchtown and a pub at Bridge.

The directions are given from the main car park overlooking the beach at Portreath, but roadside parking is usually available near Illogan parish church if you prefer, or you might care to seek permission to use the car park at the Bridge Inn.

See the note about Walks 11-15 on page 114.

1 From the car park's main entrance, cross the road and turn left along the lane leading to the Basset Arms, taking the narrow path on the left at the entrance to the pub car park. The walk route continues past the pub, along the footpath beside the stream, with a long terrace of old cottages on the right, some very tiny. The bridge ahead carries the Incline, and when you reach it it's worth looking up to the right to see the huge granite retaining wall that was built to support it.

THE PORTREATH INCLINE
It was cut through solid rock in 1837-8 as part of the Hayle Railway, which linked the Camborne and Redruth mines to the ports of Hayle and Portreath. Several rails ran from both sides of the harbour, and horses drew wagons (usually loaded with coal) to the foot of the Incline, where there were turntables. There the wagons were attached to ropes, and winding gear operated by a stationary steam engine at the top hauled them up. Locomotives took them on to the mines. The same process in reverse enabled copper ore to be taken down to the harbour and shipped to South Wales for smelting. Despite some nasty accidents, mainly in the first few days of its operation, the system worked well until the line was eventually closed in 1932. During World War 2 a wall was built across the Incline a few feet from the bottom. The reason is stated by Michael Tangye to have been to discourage German invaders from using it.

This photo of the foot of the Incline was taken in 1934, two years after the system fell out of use. In the foreground can be seen one of the turntables.

Pass under the bridge and go on along Glenfeadon Terrace. There is a brief note about the Glenfeadon House Hotel on page 128. **Continue ahead along Primrose Terrace, which brings you to the path through Illogan Woods. At the notice forbidding motorcycles, continue ahead along the tarmacked path and through the narrow gap in a wall. You will now follow a stream through a wooded valley** - carpeted with bluebells in Maytime. **Keep to the main track all the way**, passing a few small ruined buildings on your left; there is also what seems to be an old leat. Some or all of these are relics of a small and unsuccessful mine called North Wheal Virgin which worked early last century. The most noticeable remains of a building come just after the track crosses the stream, and the tiny, ochre-stained stream which flows into the main one a few yards further on probably issues from the mine's adit.

This area was much used by the Bassets of Tehidy for pheasant shooting: there is an Iron Age hill-fort at Nance, just above the wood to the east, where shooting parties would lie in wait while the beaters went to work. In 1899 the *West Briton* reported, "Mr Basset's party had good sport last week. On Tuesday they killed 703 pheasants, on Wednesday 785 and on Thursday 1,109."

Still continue ahead at the point where another path is signed to the right.

When you emerge into the open you have a glimpse of Illogan church tower ahead. As you approach the road you have Nance Pond on your left and the well-manicured lawns of the Aviary Court Hotel on your right. Aviary Court, otherwise called Aviary Cottage, was the home of the highly inventive James Tangye, one of a family of well-known engineers, towards the end of the 19th century. For a little more about the Tangye family, and James's brother Richard in particular, see *Exploring Cornwall's Tramway Trails*, Volume 1, pages 151-3. The grandchildren of the engineering brothers include Nigel Tangye of Glendorgal, Newquay, and the prolific author Derek Tangye, whose writings mostly focused on his home between Lamorna and Porthcurno.

2 At the road turn left. It's a pretty little country road, which soon brings you to Illogan Church Town. (The name refers to the church's patron saint, and is pronounced "Il-**lugg**-'n" or even just "**Lugg**'n".)

3 At the road junction just beyond the Well Being Centre and primary school, turn left to continue the walk ... But first I suggest you enter the churchyard via the gateway almost opposite.

ILLOGAN CHURCH & ITS GRAVEYARD

The main body of the medieval church was demolished and replaced by a new building in the 1840s. The original intention was to take down the tower and reconstruct it as part of the new church, but Trinity House insisted that it must stay where it had always been because it was an important landmark for seafarers. It used to be whitewashed for that reason.

There are many interesting old gravestones such as the one (just left of the entrance to the churchyard as you came in) commemorating two of the six sons of Wm Willoughby, both of whom died in Ballarat, an Australian mining town, one in 1859, the other in 1861. Their father was probably the Wm Willoughby who paid 3s. 4d. to the parish in 1830 for "Portreath Stamping Mill" and dues to the Basset family of £4.6.3 in 1832 for "Copper Ore found on the beach at Portreath."

A man of note (pun not intended) in the history of Cornish music-making is buried near the north-west corner of the graveyard: Thomas

Merritt (1862-1908), without whose characteristic settings of Christmas hymns no carol concert in these parts would be complete.

Notice the ancient Celtic cross, about 20 yards south-west of the tower; it used to serve as a "station" for outdoor processions. Arthur Langdon in "Old Cornish Crosses" (1896) reports that the sexton had dug to a depth of five feet without finding the bottom of the shaft.

The new church is usually locked, though I'm told it's normally open between 2pm and 4pm on Friday afternoons. It contains several items salvaged from the old church, notably the Norman font, several carved bench-ends, and memorials to the Bassets and other important local families.

At the next road junction, where the Church Town Mini-Market is almost opposite, turn left, following the sign to Portreath.

4 After about 100m turn left again, on to a signed public footpath which starts immediately past the last of the older cottages. The hedge is on your right at first, then on your left when you have crossed the first of several granite cattle grids, known in these parts as "Cornish stiles". Now you have a wide panorama ranging from Nancekuke and St Agnes Beacon to Carn Marth (recognisable by the Pennance Mine engine house on its right-hand slope); the castle and monument on Carn Brea can just be glimpsed above the houses behind you. **After the next cattle grid, beside a power-line pole, the path turns right, then left, to run around the edge of the field, soon bringing you back to the power-line. Here cross another grid and continue straight down the slope, with a fence on your left at first. After a kissing-gate, the path runs in a slight hollow, among trees and brambles. A second kissing-gate and one last grid and you are at the road in Bridge hamlet, with the Bridge Inn on your left.**

5 Turn left past the pub, and at the main Redruth-Portreath road left again (care needed: this is a busy and rather narrow road). After less than 50 yards cross and turn sharp-right on an uphill path - not the steep drive, but the gentler one signed "Portreath Tramroad"; then turn sharp-left at the granite post bearing the engine-house logo which indicates the Mineral Tramways "Coast-to-Coast" trail.

You are now on the path which occupies the former trackbed of the Portreath Tramroad. It runs straight back to Portreath, crossing a minor road at one point.

A little information about the Tramroad is in the note about Portreath on pages 115-6; for a much fuller account, see *Exploring Cornwall's Tramway Trails* Volume 2.

The new-looking South West Water buildings, one on the right and the other down on the other side of the road, mark the point where, in 1931, the "Red River" flowing from the Carn Brea / Redruth mining district, together with the sewage outfall from Redruth and Illogan, was diverted into a thousand-feet-long tunnel to flow into the sea further north than before (at what Michael Tangye calls "an inaccessible cove"), thus avoiding or at least greatly reducing pollution of Portreath beach. By the same token, of course, it put paid to any tin-streaming operations in the village. One of the tall ventilation pipes at the back of the building on the right clearly dates from that period. ("Red Rivers" used to be a common feature of the Cornish landscape: see the note about them on page 147.) The water that still flows across Portreath beach mostly if not entirely comes from the stream you walked beside in the woods.

At the end of the path, where it becomes Sunnyvale Road, notice the "setts" (granite blocks to which the rails were attached).

WALK 15
BASSET'S COVE, THE CLIFFS, PORTREATH, ILLOGAN WOODS & TEHIDY COUNTRY PARK
About 5½ miles (9km)
The sketch map for this route is on page 114.

This is a splendidly varied walk, featuring both woodland and spectacular cliffs. No road walking is involved, apart from a very little in Portreath. There are likely to be muddy patches in the woods. The cliff path between Basset's or Bassett's Cove and Portreath involves steep descents and climbs at two deep valleys. After Portreath you are well away from toilets, pubs and shops.

If you are dependent on public transport, you will need to start the walk at Portreath (point 4 in the directions). For those with cars, however, I think the best place to begin is at Basset's Cove, west of Portreath (Grid Reference: SW 638 442). By starting there you do the toughest bit of walking first, then have an opportunity to get refreshments at Portreath and maybe relax awhile on the beach. To drive to Basset's Cove from Camborne or Redruth it's best to make for Portreath first and then take the coast road south-west towards Hayle. The rough track leading to the cliffs (not signposted, so easy to miss) is about 1½ miles by road from Portreath. There is parking space at the cliff end of the track, and also at the Tehidy Country Park's North Cliff Car Park, on the left a few yards further along the road. Another possibility would be to use the East Lodge car park, which is about 200 yards north of the East Lodge main entrance to the Park. In that case, start the walk at point 6.

See the note about Walks 11-15 on page 114.

1 Basset's Cove is named after the family that once owned, as far as I know, every inch of ground covered by this walk, plus a good deal of many of the other routes in this book: the Bassets of Tehidy. Portreath itself was once known as Basset's Cove, and this place was called Spratting Cove until the 1880s. Spratting Cove was a favourite recreation area for the Bassets, who built a summerhouse there.

Turn right along the coastal footpath when you reach the cliffs, soon crossing a stile. If you have a good head for heights, it's worth taking some of the side-paths to the cliff-edge to get a better view of the splendid scenery, such as Samphire Island ahead, whose name suggests that people used to go out there gathering samphire for pickling.

138

The view back over the beach at Basset's Cove, with Navax Point and the Godrevy Lighthouse on the skyline. In the middle distance are Crane Islands, and the small notch at the seaward edge of the headland above them is a ditch and rampart, parts of the Iron Age Crane Castle. (See page 154.)

(Remember the imaginary clifftop scene that Edgar conjures up for his blind father in *King Lear*?

"Half way down

Hangs one that gathers samphire, dreadful trade!")

Soon come the two steep descents and climbs at Porth-Cadjack Cove. The name is, I'm told, often said locally as "Scradjick"; what it means I don't know. In the earlier years of last century contraband, mainly brandy, was often landed at Porth-Cadjack, hidden in a cave and after dark hauled up by pulley to be stored at Trengove Farm (which you will pass later), before delivery to hotels in Camborne and Pool. An earlier name for this cove was Polscatha, meaning boat pool or - as with Portscatho on the south coast - boat cove.

As you go up the steps on the second climb, look back to see the waterfall; in fact there were three waterfalls in January, but the two smaller ones usually dry up in summer. The valley leading down to the cove is a fine place to watch hawks. This area is called Carvannel Downs; "Carvannel", the name of the nearby farm, seems to mean "fort of the broom-plants", but I can't say I've ever noticed either fort or broom up here. Carvannel Downs is especially rich in plant life: Rose Lewis, the former Mineral Tramways Officer, tells me that the rare, yellow-flowered dyer's greenweed (sometimes called brummel in Cornwall) and "wonderful scented burnet rose" bloom here in June, and "spring is a glory", with squill, violets, primroses, scurvy grass, thrift, blackthorn, kidney vetch, sea carrot, birdsfoot trefoil and many more, including the inevitable gorse and bluebells; later, bell heather, ling, betony and devil's bit or devil's button: a Cornish tradition was that if you picked it the Devil would come to your bedside by night. In the autumn look for field mushrooms and parasol mushrooms.

As you approach Western Cove, with its red cliffs, you may notice the group of tall masts and a large spherical building on the clifftop in the distance; this is at RAF Portreath, otherwise known as the Nancekuke Defence Area: see page 120.

Now comes the most dramatic scenery on this walk, the long, narrow promontory known as The Horse - best seen, I always feel when I'm there, by lying prone on the clifftop and peering cautiously down. A photograph and some comments about it and Ralph's Cupboard, the gulley on the left, are on pages 125-6.

2 As you approach Portreath, fork right down into the valley for the easy route, or take one of the more strenuous paths to the left round or over Western Hill. (For details about routes and points of interest, again see pages 125-6.)

3 At the bottom of the valley path is Smugglers' Cottage.

Smugglers' Cottage once belonged to the Bassets, and descriptions are extant from about 1810 of Miss Frances Basset bathing in troughs with steps inside, still to be seen on the cliff face near the small cave. There are five of them, some with plugholes. The house, reputed to have been originally a fish cellar, is unlikely in fact to have been the scene of much smuggling, because for a long time the "Preventative Men" or "Preventives" were based at Portreath; indeed, the other name by which it is often known, Amy's or Amey's Cottage, apparently alludes to one Amy Jeffrey who lived there, and she was a Preventive officer's widow! Even so, there is good evidence that a tunnel led from behind a large fireplace in the cottage to a cave below ...

A possible route from here at low tide is to cross the beach and walk up from the car park to the Basset Arms. The route I would recommend, though, is to take the road above. This gives you a good view over the western side of the beach, known as Carvannel Cove.

The first harbour at Portreath was built on this side in 1713 to serve the needs of the mines. A quay jutted out 150 feet from the small headland known as "Point" or "Amy's Point", and goods presumably had to be winched to and from a clifftop track, rather like the system at Trevaunance, St Agnes. (Again, see Walk 12 for a little more about this, and Walk 8 for information about St Agnes harbour.) As at St Agnes, storms soon destroyed this harbour, but its foundations are still there. Autumn gales exposed them for a while in 1983, and there is an interesting photograph of them in Michael Tangye's *Tehidy and the Bassets*.

Overlooking the beach is the castellated Battery House. At this place in 1782 a battery of four 12-pound cannons was erected to protect the cove from attacks by privateers and the French. Two more cannons were positioned by the entrance to the new harbour on the east side. Only once were they fired in earnest, when a French ship in difficulties entered the harbour and was captured; otherwise they were in action only for ceremonial occasions such as the opening of the Portreath Tramroad. A cannon dated 1789 used to stand in the yard beside Battery House, but has a new home now in the forecourt of the Portreath Arms. Most other remains of the battery also seem to have gone, but you can still just see where a cave was cut into the cliff, possibly as a gunpowder store. The entrance has been partially blocked now, and a concrete-block garage built in front of it. A few little castellated walls in the cliff above Battery House have also survived.

Continue down to the main road.

4 Cross the road and continue ahead, taking the narrow path on the left at the entrance to the Basset Arms car park. Now continue as described in section 1 of Walk 14 (pages 133-5).

5 At the road turn right, passing a restored pump and mounting block. Soon on the left comes Glebe Farm, attractively restored and renamed "The Barnyard". Continue along the minor road to the T-junction, and there turn right on to a somewhat busier road.

The point immediately beyond a pair of 40mph speed-restriction signs, where the road bends slightly left, is where the Portreath Branch of the Hayle Railway crossed. You can still see where it ran: on the right a grassy lane beyond a wooden farm gate, and on the left a narrower path. **Here take another narrow path, which continues almost in the same line as you have been walking along the road. It starts with the remains of an iron kissing-gate just to the left of the entrance to a house. The path runs beside garden walls and fences for almost its entire length - nearly half a mile - and is fairly straight apart from one right-then-left manoeuvre, where there are footpath signs.**

On reaching a wide lane, turn left, and then at the road cross and turn left again. Take care - the traffic along here tends to be speedy. 6 Turn right to enter the Tehidy Country Park at the East Lodge gate. (If you are basing this walk on the East Lodge car park, start by walking to the East Lodge main entrance by following the path - on your left as you enter the car park - which runs more-or-less parallel with the road. Turn right along the main drive.)

THE BASSETS & THEIR TEHIDY ESTATE

Tehidy (said with a short i-sound, "Tehiddy") was the home of the Basset family (the Lords de Dunstanville), who were leading lights in the industrial development of Portreath, Camborne and Redruth. They acquired the Manor of Tehidy about 1150 when William Basset married into the de Dunstanville family. By 1330 they had built a large house, probably replaced in Tudor times. Mining ventures brought them great wealth by the early years of the 18th century, and work on a fine new mansion, together with a park, gardens and a lake, was started in 1734. A windbreak of trees to the north was planted, and when this was established sub-tropical shrubs were imported for the gardens. Special roads and carriageways were built.

In 1779 Francis Basset earned royal favour by leading a small army of Cornish miners to Plymouth to help strengthen defences against French or Spanish invasion, and was rewarded by being made a baronet. In 1796 he became Baron de Dunstanville, and in 1797 Baron Basset of Stratton. His funeral in 1835 was probably the grandest ever seen in Cornwall, and in the following year the monument on Carn Brea was erected in his honour. Michael Tangye's "Tehidy and the Bassets" tells in some detail of the family's wealth, industrial enterprises, and "good works" such as building local schools and distributing charity.

By the end of the 19th century the Basset fortunes were on the wane, largely because their income from the mines fell dramatically but their lifestyle remained extravagant: Arthur, for example, who inherited in 1888, gambled heavily at the races and spent lavishly on his own racehorses. He passed much of his time at other Basset properties "up-country", and Tehidy became increasingly neglected. In 1915 the mansion was finally vacated, and in 1916 the manors and farms were sold off.

The new owners of Tehidy offered the house (plus 250 acres of the park) for sale at £10,000 for use as a chest hospital, and in January 1919 the first five TB patients were admitted. Hardly a month later, a mysterious fire devastated most of the main building. With the help of insurance money, a new, purpose-built hospital was completed by 1922.

The 250-acre estate was bought in 1983 by Cornwall County Council and has been developed into an attractive woodland park with over nine miles of footpaths, some suitable for wheelchairs, and three miles of bridleways. Health Service cuts led to the closure of Tehidy Hospital, and most of the buildings have been converted into apartments.

Continue ahead along the main drive, through woods at first, then beside the golf links. A pictorial map of the country park, showing paths and main features of interest, is beside a seat overlooking the golf course. The choice of paths and tracks within the park is even greater and more confusing than the map implies; the following directions attempt to guide you by the most direct and clear route.

You now enter what is still called the Pine Walk, and indeed young pines have been planted on both sides, but the great trees that used to line it have gone now, felled by the County Council on the grounds of old age, and nothing remains of them but their sawn-off stumps, most of them now a riot of fungi. One of the better-preserved ones seems to have had a spiral pattern carved into it, and at the far end of the avenue one fallen trunk has been converted into a couple of seats. A sketch and photograph overleaf give some idea of how the scene has changed.

7 **Immediately after you pass through two kissing-gates into more woodland, a sign directs you to the North Cliffs Circular Walk by following the wooden posts with a pink-painted groove cut into them. Turn right, therefore. The path eventually brings you to a small clearing with a seat on the right. Take the next right turning. This winding path eventually takes you past another seat. At the "crosspaths" turn right again - though surprisingly there is no pink waymark post here to tell you so. Ignore the next path on the left. Where at least five**

paths meet and the large sign directs you to the left, still go straight on for Basset's Cove. (Turning left would bring you to the North Cliffs Car Park.) Soon you leave the wood. From this point it's worth looking back at the profile of the woodland, shaped by the salt sea winds, with low scrub at the edge, diminutive sycamore and old coppiced beech woods next, then rather taller oak and ash, and finally big specimens of beech and other trees furthest inland. **After two stone cattle-grids and a wooden stile you will reach the main coast road. The track down to Basset's Cove is a few yards away to your left.**

Tehidy Country Park: the Pine Walk as it was in 1989 (left), and in 2005, following replanting

WALK 16
BASSET'S COVE, TEHIDY COUNTRY PARK, THE RED RIVER, HELL'S MOUTH AND THE COAST PATH
About 8 miles

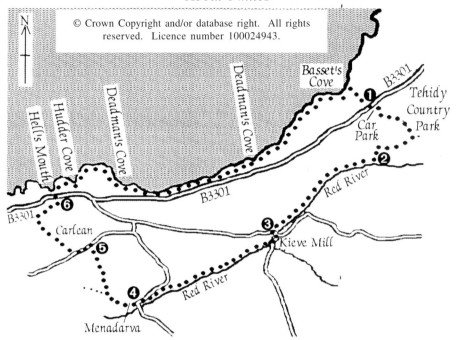

This is one of the easier walks described in this book, in the sense that the going is on the level except between points 4 and 6 on the map, and even there you have very little climbing to do. On the other hand, you do need to prepare for mud, probably even during lengthy dry spells, and again it's the western inland section of the walk that presents the worst problems - notably as you leave Menadarva and as you enter woodland on the approach to Hell's Mouth. The path between points 5 and 6 is for the most part badly maintained. As the map shows, you could avoid all these difficulties by using the minor roads, but this entails a few hundred yards along the B3301, which tends to carry quite a lot of traffic. Personally I'd strongly recommend the footpaths route, even if that means wearing wellies for the whole walk.

Please don't let any of that put you off. It's a splendid walk: beautiful woodland for much of the inland section; fine panoramic views at the western end; and awe-inspiring cliff scenery along the coast. Ideally placed at the half-way point is the Hell's Mouth Café, which has a good selection of hot and cold refreshments on sale daily from Easter to late October, and on most fine Sundays during the winter Colin Trezise is there to serve hot drinks, sweets - and ice-cream for the hardy.

Directions are given from the car park at the North Cliffs entrance to Tehidy Country Park. For details on how to find it, see the introduction to Walk 15. If that car park is full, as it often is on pleasant days because of the popularity of the Country Park, try the larger one on the cliff-edge overlooking Basset's Cove: the rough road leading to it is almost opposite the Tehidy car park entrance. Failing that, if you drive on westwards you will see several other small parking spaces on the seaward side of the road, and the Hell's Mouth Café has its own car park which is frequently used by walkers. Mr Trezise does not insist that they be customers, but obviously their custom would be appreciated.

1 Go through the gap beside the gate at the inland end of the Tehidy car park, and now keep to the main track. (The many side paths are very tempting, but if I send you along any of them you're most likely to lose your way.) A felled tree beside the track is shown in the photo.

At the first major T-junction keep left, following the route indicated by wooden poles with pale pink (almost white) markings. This soon brings you to another T-junction: ahead are houses, and gates marked "Private Access, Residents Only". Here turn right, walking at first beside the fence, and at the signpost turn left, following the "Otter Bridge, Lake" sign.

2 Immediately before the bridge, turn right along West Drive. (But if you want to see the lake first, and/or call at the café, cross the bridge and turn left, later returning the same way. Another attractive possibility would be to follow the sign to Oak Wood, and from there you could cut back to West Drive further west.) The bridge spans what is still known as the Red River, though it's no more than a stream and it's no longer red; and at least the next two miles of the walk route runs beside it, even though for much of the time it's neither visible nor audible.

RED RIVERS

This is not the only Cornish stream to be so named: another flows through Redruth and met the sea at Portreath until it was diverted early in the 1930s (see pages 125 and 137), and that one must have been discoloured by mine waste from very early times, because the name "Redruth" means "red ford". (Just to confuse you, it's the "ruth" part of the word that means "red"!)

Soon after this stream further west begins its journey to the sea it flows through the Tuckingmill valley, where some of Cornwall's greatest mines were, including Dolcoath and Cook's Kitchen, and till recently South Crofty, so for several centuries its modern name was quite literally true. I'm not sure how recently it lost its colour, but I can remember being startled by its redness when I first saw it in the mid-1960s. "Like tomato ketchup," according to the editor of a local newspaper - and I can confirm that from personal experience, since my home overlooks Restronguet Creek, between Truro and Falmouth: many readers will remember the "Wheal Jane Disaster" of January 1992, when millions of gallons of mine water gushed into the Carnon River. On meeting salt water the iron oxide in it was precipitated, turning the creek bright orange. (The heavy metals, such as zinc and cadmium, were invisible but far more dangerous. For a fuller account, see "Tramway Trails" Volume 2, pages 168-9.)

After nearly a mile of attractive woodland - delightful on the sunny February day when I was last there, even though the bluebells and primroses were not yet on show - **the path gradually emerges into the open.** Here there is a camp site down to the left, and the stream runs along the far side of it.

At Magor Farm, on higher ground nearby to the south, are the remains of a small "Roman-style" villa dating back to about 150 AD. They were partially excavated in the 1930s but are now buried again. The house may have been built by a local man who had lived "up-country" for a time and grown used to Roman architecture: there are few if any signs that Romans themselves settled this far west.

3 On reaching the road at Bell Lake, turn left, cross the bridge, then turn right.

BELL LAKE

Where's the lake? you may be wondering. As far as I know, there isn't one. In an article in "Cornish Archaeology" (1971) Michael Tangye offers an interesting explanation. An old Cornish name for this place may have been "cum helyk", "valley of the willows", and "cum helyk" has become "Combellack", a fairly common Cornish surname. Coombe is just a few yards north of Bell Lake, so Mr Tangye's theory seems very probably correct. Incidentally, my wife knows this place as Kieve Mill; Kieve Mill Farm is nearby, but nowadays the mill seems to be as absent as the lake.

Next follow the Public Bridleway sign, crossing the stream again via a wide wooden bridge. A notice welcomes you to the Red River Valley Local Nature Reserve, and now for another mile-or-so you are walking with the stream on your left. Horses, and apparently also sometimes tractors and other vehicles, use this track, so it's likely to be boggy in places, but in February we found we could easily skirt the various pools and puddles. **Eventually you will come to another wide wooden bridge, but don't cross that. Soon afterwards the path curves right, crosses a tributary stream by means of stepping stones, and meets a minor road.**

4 If you are unwilling to tackle the mud and other likely complications on the footpaths between here and Hell's Mouth, as described in the introductory comments, turn right and keep to the roads. Ignore the first left turning, turn left at the T-junction, and on joining the main

coast road (B3301) continue ahead (or left). Please take special care here: walk facing oncoming traffic, and go up on to the bank where possible.

But for the route shown on my map, turn left. Where the road bends left, go straight ahead, following a Public Footpath sign. The wide drive soon takes you past the ancient-looking Menadarva Barton and its outbuildings.

MENADARVA

The name derives from Mertherderwa, the chapel or shrine of Derwa or Derwe, a Virgin Saint, one of several Irish missionaries reputed to have landed at Hayle along with St Gothian, from whom Gwithian takes its name. Nothing seems to have survived of any such chapel, but references to it or its ruined remains are in documents ranging from 1447 to 1925, and a font taken from it, probably about 900 years old, is now in the church at Tuckingmill, Camborne. Professor Charles Thomas believes the chapel may well have been very close or even attached to Menadarva Barton. Back in 1990 Mr James Olds, the owner, very kindly showed me over the house, one room of which is lined with oak panelling. He believed parts of the house to date from the 13th century; certainly there is some Tudor work in it, such as the mullioned windows now built into the nearby shed. These must be relics of the house built by the Arundell family, whose main seat was Lanherne at St Mawgan (see "Around Newquay", Walk 2). Most of what is now seen presumably dates from the 18th century, when the property was acquired by the Bassets of Tehidy (1755). Notice the pigeon-holes in one wall of the house. Another remarkable sight at Menadarva fifteen years ago was Mr Olds's favourite hunting horse, Trelawney; I was assured he was one of the finest horses of all time, and was still fighting fit at the ripe age of 40.

The path now continues ahead, via the farm gate. On the far side of it in February cattle were feeding, and the ground was churned up into a morass. My wife and I made the mistake of crossing the centre of it and almost got permanently stuck while the cows looked on with what Stephanie assures me was a glint in the eye; it helps if walkers can see the funny side, too. I suspect that we'd have been better advised to skirt the morass via the hedge on the left at first ... Now head uphill to where you will see a pair of farm gates. Go through the right-hand one and

then walk beside the hedge on your right. From various points now you get wide views inland including Carn Brea, the hill with a "castle" and tall monument on top - a place very closely associated with the Bassets of Tehidy. (For information about it and a walk exploring it, see pages 90-95 in *Tramway Trails* Volume 1.) The tall chimney stack you may glimpse in a valley to the south is the one you see as you drive through the "Roseworthy Dip" on the A30; it belonged to an arsenic works. A little later, the view westwards features St Ives Bay, with Carbis Bay on the far side and Knill's Monument on the skline. (For that, see *A View from Trencrom*, Walk 8.) **Cross the low stile with a metal bar over it at the top corner of the field and continue ahead as before.** Hereabouts we were delighted to hear the songs of several skylarks high overhead - quite a rarity these days. **Another stile brings you to a country road.**

5 Turn left on that. After a short distance there are two large farm buildings on the left, and on the right a few yards beyond them was, in February 2005, a broken-down farm gate, laced with barbed wire. This is where the path to Hell's Mouth starts. Thanks partly to thorny growth on the left, opening the gate was more of a problem than straddling it at the lowest point; I hope that before too long steps will be taken to improve access to the path. **Again walk beside the hedge on your right and go through another farm gate** - in much better condition, but again hard to open, this time because it is attached to a wooden pallet, so you might prefer to climb it (at the hinge end, please). **Now the path descends quite steeply to a patch of woodland. On the edge of it is a small wooden gate, on both sides of which the ground is extremely boggy, but with care you should be able to bypass the worst of it. A few makeshift stepping-stones help with crossing the two little streams. After that the path runs more-or-less straight ahead to the far side of the wood,** where there is a house with its attendant outbuildings - a washhouse and outside toilet - all of them currently uninhabited and what estate agents refer to as an ideal opportunity for the home handyman, but by the time you walk here they may have been restored to use by their owner, Mr Trezise (who runs the café nearby). He told us the house was formerly two cottages for gamekeepers employed by the Tehidy estate. **From the house a wide track runs up, along the edge of the wood, and after a metal farm gate you turn left, over the remains of a stile, and walk beside the café.**

6 Probably you'll want to linger there for refreshments. **When you're ready, cross the road with care and - with even more care unless you have a very good head for heights - take a look at Hell's Mouth, "a sheer drop of 200 feet" as a card on sale at the café points out.**

The view westwards from near Hell's Mouth: Navax Point in the distance

HELL'S MOUTH

Hell's Mouth is a popular tourist attraction, and not only because of its lurid name and the closeness of the coast road. Here and at nearby Hudder Cove the sea is working away at patches of rock slightly softer than the rest. The results provide opportunities not only for the suicidally inclined but also for illicit dumpers of rubbish.

The fearful reputation of this stretch of coast is confirmed by the fact that two places between Hell's Mouth and Portreath are called Deadman's Cove. Probably Hell's Mouth was named by sailors; it has been the graveyard of a good many ships, the most recent of which was the Panamanian-registered freighter "Secil Japan". After her cargo of timber shifted in high winds she was driven on to the rocks a little way to the east shortly before midnight on 12th March 1989. Two Sea King helicopters carried out a rescue operation with the aid of car headlamps on the cliff-edge; all twelve crew were lifted off, but one fell out of the harness and drowned. *"As the man got near us,"* reported one of the helicopter winchmen, *"he opened his arms, slipped away, and fell 200 feet into the sea."* The remains of the ship were still to be seen nearly a year later, when I originally researched this walk.

Above: The wreck of the "Secil Japan" as seen from Hell's Mouth (January 1990).

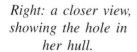

Right: a closer view, showing the hole in her hull.

Turn right. From here to Basset's Cove is simply a matter of following the coastal footpath, and directions are superfluous. Despite several more awe-inspiring drops to sea or rocks below, the path itself is relatively level and featureless, but the long views in both directions are splendid. Look back to see the famous Godrevy lighthouse.

Photo by Stephanie Acton

Godrevy Point and Island take their name from the nearby farm, meaning "smallholdings". The island marks the landward end of a mile-long reef usually called The Stones, but since nine rocks are visible at low tide they were once known locally as The Nine Maidens. Many ships have been wrecked on them; the best-known example is the "Garland", which when she sank in January 1649 was carrying clothing and other property of the recently-beheaded Charles I. Many valuable items were washed ashore, and rumours of a vast treasure on the sea-bed still attract the occasional diver.

The growth of Hayle's importance as a port because of the mines led to a great increase in the number of wrecks during the 18th and 19th centuries, and when a particularly large death toll resulted from the loss of the steamer "Nile" in 1854, demands for a lighthouse to be built became irresistible. The cost of putting one on the outermost rock was estimated to be £45,000, whereas the figure for a lighthouse on Godrevy Island was only £8,500, so after much controversy the latter was decided on, and the builders' actual price was even lower (£7,082 15s. 7d). Despite holdups caused by bad weather and visits by thousands of sightseers from Hayle, the work progressed, and the light shone for the first time on 1st March 1859. The lighthouse was manned by two keepers, so three were appointed, and they worked a rota of two months on and one month off. For eight stormy days in 1925 one keeper had to cope alone because his mate had been taken ill; when he eventually came to the mainland he was given a hero's welcome. In 1934 Godrevy became an unmanned lighthouse, and its light is now controlled from St Ives.

I am indebted for most of this information to Professor Charles Thomas, whose booklet about Godrevy (1985) is called "To the Lighthouse", a reference to the fact that Virginia Woolf's novel of that name was inspired by a family boat-trip from St Ives to Godrevy in 1892.

The rocky little offshore outcrops just west of Basset's Cove are called Crane Islands. They mark the far end of what was once - within the past three centuries - a promontory, the site of an Early Iron Age fortified settlement, Crane Castle. (The name is probably a corruption of Cornish "car hen", "old fort".) All trace of any dwellings has gone; what do remain are the two impressive banks and 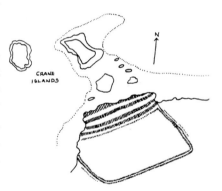 ditches which protected the "castle" from attack on the landward side, plus a large rectangular enclosure surrounded by embankments 2-3 feet high. The research which led to the discovery of this enclosure (possibly a pound for livestock?) was carried out by Michael Tangye, whose sketch plan of Crane Castle I have reproduced with his kind permission.

To find the remains, you need to take a narrow path through the gorse and heather on the left; the one I mean starts just a few yards before you get your first glimpse of the quite large car park above Basset's Cove. Almost at once the path goes over a small hump, where it crosses the embankment surrounding the enclosure. The two banks and ditches are very obvious once you reach them, and the second (inner) bank remains quite a formidable barrier even after two millennia. (See the photograph on page 139, showing the view westwards across Basset's Cove.)

SOME MINING TERMS

This book is written with the interested general reader in mind, rather than those who have made a special study of mining in Cornwall. Although some explanations of technical terms are included in the main text, I think a brief glossary may prove helpful. Please bear in mind, however, that these are very simplified explanations: several of these words have formed the basis of lengthy articles and even whole books. The illustrations in this section, apart from those of the buddle and horse whims, are taken from the Perran Foundry catalogue dating from the early 1870s, by courtesy of the Trevithick Society.

ADIT A drainage channel with its mouth or **PORTAL** in a valley or on a hillside or cliff face. In deep mines the water had to be raised by pumping to the level of the adit; this is why statistics often state the depth of a mine "below adit". Adits also often doubled as shafts by following the metal **LODE** (vein), and in some cases provided access for the miners.

BAL An area of tin-working. Mines named Bal tend to be older than those called **WHEAL** or **HUEL**, though this is certainly not a hard-and-fast rule. Oliver Padel suggests that a Bal was generally a group of workings, especially on the surface, whereas a Wheal was a specific tin-work.

BEAM ENGINE Thomas Newcomen of Dartmouth (1663-1729) was the first to develop a steam engine which could be used for pumping water up from the mines. The cylinder was placed vertically and securely bolted to a massive, usually granite, bedstone, and the piston was chained to one end of a wooden or cast iron beam or **BOB**, pivoted on a strong wall, known as the **BOB WALL**. The other end overhung the mine shaft and was attached by long rods to the pump at the bottom. In deep shafts the pitwork, as it was called, would have been too heavy for the beam to lift without the aid of at least one **BALANCE BOB.** Balance bobs were small beams with one end attached to the pump rod and the other heavily weighted: when the rod descended the balance bob's weight prevented

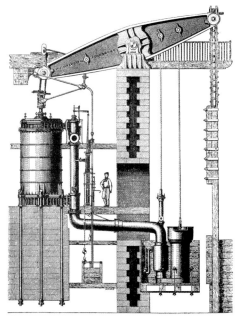

A typical large steam pumping engine. This one was made for Poldice Mine, near St Day.

it from falling too quickly, and when it rose the weight helped it up. In the 1770s James Watt and Matthew Boulton began manufacturing an improved engine, and James Pickard modified beam engines to produce rotative motion, used mainly for driving the whim and stamps. (See the entries on those.) Early in the 19th century, great improvements were brought by the use of high-pressure steam; the research and inventions of Richard Trevithick (1771-1833) made an important contribution here, but many other engineers also played a significant part. The size of each engine was expressed in terms of the diameter of its cylinder: 45", 90", etc.

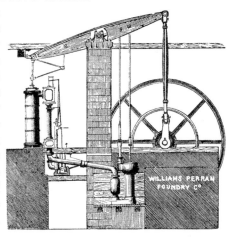

A rotative beam engine, normally used for winding or for driving stamps

BLOWING HOUSE The early form of smelting house, in which the furnace temperature was raised by bellows, usually operated by a waterwheel.

BUDDLE A device for concentrating ore by means of gravity. Early buddles were rectangular, but in the 19th century most were circular; water containing the ore

A restored convex buddle at Blue Hills Tin Streams, near St Agnes (seen on Walk 7)

which had been reduced to a fine powder in the stamps was fed to the centre of a **CONVEX BUDDLE** or the sides of a **CONCAVE** one, and rotating brushes were used to ensure that the heaviest, metal-bearing particles settled closest to the inlet point. A more sophisticated form of buddle called a **ROUND FRAME** came into use in Cornwall in the 1870s. In this the bowl rather than the brushes rotated.

BURNING HOUSE or **CALCINER** (pronounced "cal-sign-er") A furnace in which ore was roasted in order to drive off impurities such as arsenic and sulphur. If the arsenic was wanted, the fumes were passed though a long, zigzag flue known as a **LAMBRETH** (labyrinth), from which the deposits were collected.

BURROW or **DUMP** A heap of mine waste (**GANGUE, HALVANS, DEADS** or **ATTLE**) - often very useful now as evidence of the mine's production. The burrows of many old mines have been "worked over" for valuable minerals which can be recovered by improved techniques.

SOME MINING TERMS

COFFIN, COFFEN or **GOFFEN** One of many terms used for mining on the surface. A coffin or **GUNNIS** is a narrow, slot-like excavation; where a broader, quarry-like pit was dug the term used was **OPENWORK** or **BEAM**. The word **STOPE** normally means an excavated area underground, but is also sometimes used of surface workings.

COUNT HOUSE The mine's office.

DRESSING FLOOR The area where the ore was prepared for smelting.

DRIVE A level (horizontal excavation).

DRY A building where mine workers changed their clothes; some dries also had washing and/or bathing facilities.

FATHOM Six feet.

FLAT-RODS Wooden or (usually) iron rods which were used to transfer power from a steam engine or waterwheel to a remote location.

LEAT An artificial watercourse. Where a leat was carried in a raised trough it was known as a **LAUNDER**.

MAN ENGINE An apparatus for raising and lowering men in a shaft, first used in Cornwall during the 1840s. Steps and hand-holds were fixed to a rod, or in some cases two rods, connected to an engine at surface. At Levant, which used the single-rod type, there were fixed platforms, about 18" square, at corresponding intervals in the shaft so that by stepping from rod to fixed platform or vice-versa at the instant they became level with one another, a miner could go up or down.

OLD MEN'S SHAFTS / WORKINGS Mines or pits which pre-date existing records; this usually means, before the mid-18th century.

SETT "The ground granted to a company of adventurers" (C. C. James) (**ADVENTURERS** were shareholders in a mining enterprise, but with unlimited liability.) The word "sett" was also used for the granite blocks used to carry rails.

STAMPS Cornish Stamps machines were used to crush the small lumps of ore into material like sand in texture. Heavy timber or iron lifters with iron "heads" at the bottom were raised by cams on a rotating axle, and fell on the ore, fed into a box beneath. Small stamps were usually powered by water-wheels, as in the picture, and larger ones by steam engines. **CALIFORNIAN STAMPS** began to supersede the Cornish variety late in the 19th century. Developed in the Californian gold-fields, they  employed heavier heads, which rotated, thus reducing wear and enabling a much greater output of crushed ore.

STREAMING The normal method of winning tin before deep mining became possible. **ALLUVIAL TIN** washed down into valleys and buried under silt was exposed, originally by shovel and barrow; the tin-bearing gravel was then sorted and washed, and the waste material used to back-fill the excavated area. Nowadays, earth-movers and lorries do the work.

TAILINGS DAM / RESERVOIR In modern tin mines, the waste material, mixed with water, is pumped into a reservoir and allowed to settle; eventually the water may be re-used by the mine, and the tailings are sometimes re-processed at a later date when conditions make this worthwhile. Finally - at least in theory - the dried-out reservoir is grassed over.

TRIBUTER A miner who contracted to work for a limited time. (The Cornish miners prided themselves on their independence, and were reluctant to become mere employees.)

WHIM A machine for raising or lowering ore or other heavy materials - and sometimes men. The earliest whims were operated by human beings or horses, walking round and round a flat circular area called a **WHIM PLAT** turning a wooden drum or capstan, around which was wound the cable attached to the **KIBBLE** or bucket. Some **HORSE WHIMS** continued in use till the 20th century, but the whims in deep mines were driven by steam engines. An improvement on kibbles were the steel containers called **SKIPS**; these were sometimes equipped with wheels and drawn up and down the rails of a **SKIP ROAD**.

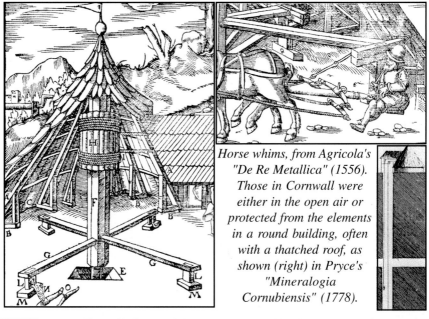

Horse whims, from Agricola's "De Re Metallica" (1556). Those in Cornwall were either in the open air or protected from the elements in a round building, often with a thatched roof, as shown (right) in Pryce's "Mineralogia Cornubiensis" (1778).

WINZE "A small ventilating shaft between two levels" (Chambers) Winzes were also sometimes used for access.

FURTHER READING

Acton, Bob: *Exploring Cornwall's Tramway Trails* (2 volumes); *A History of Truro Volume 3: Exploring the City - and Around; Around Newquay; Around the River Fowey* and *From the Roseland to St Austell Bay* are the Landfall books currently in print that most closely relate to historical details in this book. See also Brown, Kenneth, below.

Andrew, Robert: *The History of RAF Perranporth 1941-45* (Penwartha, 1995; 2nd edition, 2000)

Anon: *The Four Churches of Perranzabuloe* (attractive booklet available in the parish church and St Michael's, Perranporth; no details given of author, publisher or date - but quite recent)

Atkinson, Barry: *Mining Sites in Cornwall and South West Devon* (Truran, 1988)

Bennett, Alan: *Images of Cornwall* (Runpast Publishing, 1992)

Benney, Clive: *St Agnes Parish, 1850-1920* (Clive Benney / Diversions Ltd, no date); *St Agnes Parish, 1920-1950* (Clive Benney, 1988); and *Around St Agnes* (Chalford, 1996)

Benney, Clive & Mansell, Tony: *A History of Blackwater and its Neighbours* (Trelease, 2004)

Bizley, M.H.: *Friendly Retreat: The Story of a Parish* (1955, reprinted by the St Agnes Museum Trust, 1994); also, *A Portrait of a Village Church: The Parish Church of Saint Agnes, in the County of Cornwall, England* (Original now scarce, but a typed transcript may be available in the church)

Brown, Kenneth, and Acton, Bob: *Exploring Cornish Mines*, Volume 1 (for Wheal Kitty, Blue Hills and Tywarnhayle mines); Volume 3 (for East Wheal Rose, Polberro, Trevaunance and West Kitty mines); Volume 4 (for Wheal Coates and the mines around Chapel Porth); and Volume 5 for updates. (All published by Landfall)

Buckley, J.A.: *Cornish Mining - at Surface* (Tor Mark Press, 1990)

Bullen, L.J.: *Mining in Cornwall*, Volumes 4 & 5 (Tempus, 2001 & 2002)

Carpenter, Frank: *St Agnes 1001-1999, A Millennium Chronicle* (St Agnes Museum, 2000)

Collins, J. H.: *Observations on the West of England Mining Region* (1912; Cornish Mining Classics, 1988)

Dines, H.G.: *The Metalliferous Mining Region of South-West England* (HMSO, 1956)

Douch, H.L.: *East Wheal Rose* (Bradford Barton, 1964)

Edwards, Michael: *Perran at War* (Author, 1995)

Hattam, Derek: *Cornish Land Steam in and around Perran Parish* (Truran, 1983)

Henwood, George: *Cornwall's Mines and Miners* (1857-9, reprinted by Bradford Barton, 1972)

Jenkin, A.K.Hamilton: *The Mines and Miners of Cornwall* (c.1960-70; most recent edition by Forge Books)   Volume 2: *St Agnes to Perranporth*
Volume 7: *Perranporth to Newquay*

FURTHER READING

John, C.R.: *The Saints of Cornwall* (Dyllansow Truran, 1981)

King, John: *The Parish of St Agnes, Cornwall* (typewritten pamphlet - may be available in the church)

Landry, Ernest & Branfield, John: *Memories of Nancekuke* (Authors, 1978)

Lyon, R.T.: *Cornwall's Playing Places* (no details given of publisher or date, but post-2001)

Mansell, Tony: *Mithian* (Trelease Publications, 2003)

Marks, Ade: *A Rock and Stroll Story! (Portreath Geology Guide & Illustrated Rock Trails)* (Author, no date)

Noall, Cyril: *Cornish Mine Disasters* (Truran, 1989)

Ordish, H. G.: *Cornish Engine Houses, A Pictorial Survey* (Bradford Barton, 1967), and *Cornish Engine Houses, A Second Pictorial Survey* (same, 1968)

Padel, O.J.: *Cornish Place-Name Elements* (English Place-Name Society, 1985), and *A Popular Dictionary of Cornish Place-Names* (Alison Hodge, 1988)

Pearce, Frank: *Portrait of a Cornish Village: St Agnes* (Bantam Books, 1977)

Perranzabuloe Old Cornwall Society: *Perranzabuloe 1900-1985* (Penwartha, 1995)

Reade, Lewis: *Branch Line Memories,* Volume 1: *Great Western* (Atlantic, 1983) and *The Branch Lines of Cornwall* (same, 1984)

Sharpe, Adam: *The Red River Trail* (Cornwall Archaeological Unit, 1990)

Sharpe, Adam, and Smith, John: *Trevellas, St Agnes* and *Wheal Coates, St Agnes* (Two reports produced by the Cornwall Archaeological Unit in 1986)

St Agnes Museum Trust: Annual Journals, from 1984 to present; also *St Agnes Miners' & Mechanics' Institute, 1893-1993*

St Newlyn East Local Studies Group: *St Newlyn East, A History of the Parish* (2000); *St Newlyn East, A Pictorial View, Book 1, The Village* (2002); and *Book 2, The Parish* (2003) (last two published by Landfall)

Stanier, Peter: *Cornwall's Mining Heritage* (Twelveheads, 1988)

Stengelhofen, John: *Cornwall's Railway Heritage* (Twelveheads, 1988)

Tangye, Michael: *Portreath, Some Chapters in its History* (Author, 1968 & 1978; third edition, Truran, 1984)

Tangye, Michael: *Tehidy and the Bassets* (Truran, 1984)

Tanner, Kathy: *St Agnes and Chapel Porth* (National Trust "Coast of Cornwall" leaflet No. 8, 1987)

Thomas, Janet: *Illogan, More than a Village* (Truran, 1990)

Tomlin, E.W.F.: *In Search of St Piran* (Lodenek Press, 1982)

Tonkin, Thomas: *The Parish of St Agnes* (written c.1710-33, reprinted in the Journal of the Royal Institution of Cornwall, 1975-6)

Trembath, Bill: *Perranporth and Perranzabuloe Parish* (Lodenek Press, 1992)

Trounson, J.: *Mining in Cornwall,* Volume 2 (Moorland, no date)

Williams, H.V.: *Cornwall's Old Mines* (Tor Mark Press, no date)

Woon, Dawn: *Do You Remember Cameron Estate?* (Author, 2002) and *Memories of Peterville* (Author, 2003)